The Revolt of the Potemkin

The Revolt of the Potemkin
The Naval Revolt of 1905 Which Heralded the Russian Revolution

Constantine Feldmann

Translated by Constance Garnett

The Revolt of the Potemkin
The Naval Revolt of 1905 Which Heralded the Russian Revolution
by Constantine Feldmann
Translated by Constance Garnett

First published under the title
The Revolt of the Potemkin

Leonaur is an imprint of Oakpast Ltd

Copyright in this form © 2021 Oakpast Ltd

ISBN: 978-1-78282-968-3 (hardcover)
ISBN: 978-1-78282-969-0 (softcover)

http://www.leonaur.com

Publisher's Notes

The views expressed in this book are not necessarily those of the publisher.

Contents

The Rising in Odessa Before the Arrival of the "Potemkin" 7

The Arrival of the "Potemkin" 12

The Causes of the Mutiny 18

The First Day 34

The Second Day 48

The Third Day 64

The Fourth Day 79

Dorofy Koshuba 89

The Fifth Day 92

The Last Three Days 103

How I Left the "Potemkin" 111

Conclusion 116

My Escape from Prison 120

Appendix 167

CHAPTER 1

The Rising in Odessa Before the Arrival of the "Potemkin"

The 9th of January found the proletariat of Odessa unprepared for political action. Their voice was not heard in the general chorus of angry protest from the workmen, who went out on strike in all parts of Russia.

✶✶✶✶✶✶

On January 9, 1905—"Bloody Sunday"—the workmen of St. Petersburg, led by Father Gapon and accompanied by women and children in holiday attire, and by priests carrying crosses and holy standards, attempted to go in procession to lay their sorrows before the *Tsar* in the naive belief that he would hear and help them. The crowd, perfectly peaceable and orderly, was dispersed by soldiers with rifle-fire, many being killed and wounded.

✶✶✶✶✶✶

The industrial crisis, which followed upon the war, and which had brought the greater part of Russia to the verge of famine, had not yet reached its height in Odessa. There, too, it was beginning to be felt, and many of the manufacturers were ceasing work, but the misery of the masses was not yet so extreme as to beget the heroism of despair, and the systematic organisation of labour had made little progress among them.

The local branch of the Social Democrat party found their efforts to rouse the people to a general strike at first unavailing, but the economic conditions soon provided a more favourable field for their agitation. Though the workers still found some sort of existence possible, there was great uneasiness among them, and a growing apprehension of the complete closing of the factories. The employers were cutting the hours of labour shorter and shorter with a corresponding decrease of the daily wages. Many of the factories which had barely maintained their footing were closed altogether.

And hunger was driving thousands of workers into the streets, and bringing the courage of despair into their poverty-stricken homes.

At the same time there was a strike movement among the workpeople on purely economic grounds. The Social Democrats met this movement half-way, and undertook its organisation. Acting in cooperation with the Bund, they formed a united committee for the management of the strike. Step by step, the strike gained ground, and more and more workshops joined it.

By May the whole of Peresyp, (working-class suburb of Odessa, and centre of its manufactures), and a great part of the town itself was on strike. In many factories and workshops the employers had consented to the workpeople's demands, mostly under pressure from the police, who feared that the strike would assume a political character, and the men had returned to work. In some cases—in the railway works, for instance—the managers met the *employés'* demands halfway, and so prevented a strike.

But all this only strengthened the hands of the Social Democrats. The workmen began to feel their power, and that increased their confidence in the leadership of the party. By June almost all the works in Odessa had been affected by the strike, and the movement seemed to be dying down. But by that time the organisation and revolutionary enthusiasm of the masses had reached such a pitch that the moment seemed to have come for a political rising.

The authorities, as always, hastened the outbreak.

On some trifling pretext the police summoned delegates from the workmen on strike, and then arrested them. The whole of Peresyp rose on the instant; the workers, men and women together, formed a long procession to the police-station, and demanded the release of their comrades. The police, alarmed, released their prisoners. The crowd welcomed them with loud shouts of "Hurrah!" and marched along the principal thoroughfare of Peresyp, singing the "*Varshavianka.*"

This spontaneous outbreak showed the revolutionary temper of the masses, and the Social Democrats determined to proclaim a general strike. A series of meetings was held, and the speakers, who advocated the strike, were favourably received by the workmen. The temper of the people was rising, and the strike was fixed for June 14.

On the evening of June 12, a group of Peresyp delegates, who had met together, were arrested. The news of their arrest roused the people's anger, and on the 13th five hundred workmen assembled at the Gena works in Peresyp to consider the position.

A comrade who was present told me:

We had hardly assembled, when a police-captain rode up to the works with a company of Cossacks and ordered us to disperse." 'Release our comrades; then we will disperse,' the workmen answered. . . . A few minutes later the Cossacks were riding down upon us as we sat peaceably on the stones. 'Lads, pick up the stones,' someone shouted, and a hail of stones came flying at the Cossacks. The valiant soldiers of the Don faltered, turned, and fled in different directions pursued by the workmen. They were so terrified that they did not think about 'retreating in good order.'

The workmen were triumphant at their victory. Some of them pursued the Cossacks, others began building barricades; two tram-cars and some carts were turned over. I made an attempt to appeal to the men, and to organise their actions, but in the hubbub, I could not secure their attention.

Meantime the Cossacks were hastily making ready to open fire. I rushed up to a comrade, Medviedev, an 'illegal' who was standing near me, and asked him whether he hadn't a flag by means of which he could attract the attention of the workmen. Without a moment's hesitation he pulled a pamphlet in a red cover from his pocket, and, leaping on the barricade, brandished the red book above his head, and shouted in a loud voice: 'Comrades—'

At that instant a bullet struck him dead from the barricade.

A yell of horror broke from the crowd, which began to disperse, leaving two dead and several wounded.

The police made a rush to pick up the bodies, but the workmen rallied again, and carried off the body of Medviedev. Several men lifted him up, and carried him through the streets of the suburb.

From all the houses, factories, and workshops the working people came running out to join the mournful procession; women tore their hair, and filled the air with sobs and curses on the murderers. The wailing and moaning did not cease till the police had torn the corpses away again. . . .

All Peresyp had risen by now, and we called the crowd to a meeting. Thousands of workmen from all parts of the town streamed to it, and the soldiers who were present did not touch the crowd, and showed entire sympathy with it.

It was the first time I had seen such a majestic and mighty scene of the solidarity and brotherhood of the workers.

The oppressors trembled before the raging sea of wrath of the working class.

The same evening it was decided to declare a general strike next day by way of mourning for our murdered comrades.

On the morning of June 14 there appeared a sinister warning of murders to come. A brief notice, placarded by the governor, announced in three lines that:

> Yesterday, in a conflict between the troops and the people, two workmen were killed and three wounded; the governor calls upon peaceful citizens, for the avoidance of accidents, to abstain from joining the crowds of workmen.

Peaceful citizens are bidden not to mingle with the working people, since the latter are liable to be fired on!

At eleven o'clock in the morning the firing began; shots were fired at the workmen who had gone to "fetch away" their comrades from work. A crowd of three thousand men went to "fetch away" the men at work at the Municipal Water Supply and at the factories outside the town. They carried out this task successfully, till the police-guards drove them off by opening fire upon them. The latter were few in number, and the workmen could easily have overpowered them, but the absence of weapons of any sort disheartened the crowd, and robbed them of confidence and courage.

Striking scenes were taking place in the town where all the efforts of the workmen were directed to stopping the trams and omnibuses from running. Immense crowds of people were moving along Preobrazhensky Street, the chief thoroughfare of Odessa. All seemed in holiday mood. Spectators stood in the balconies and at the windows. Suddenly a tram-car appeared on the scene; at once thirty or forty working lads dashed at it. In a moment they unharnessed the horses; the frightened passengers hurried out of the car, and amid deafening shouts and the cheers of the spectators, the tram-car fell over in the middle of the road. The bold youths were pelted with flowers from the balconies; they caught the flowers with pride, and then scurried off before the Cossacks had time to gallop up.

The latter scarcely reached the spot before, to the delight of the public, they were called off to another place, where tram-cars had been turned off the rails in the same way.

The children of the proletariat, speaking generally, played a splendid part in this strike. Everywhere they were the first to appear, and it was pleasant to see their daring young faces and the childish hands with which, before the very eyes of the Cossacks, they overturned cars and built barricades.

The latter had sprung up already in many places It is true they were mere toy fortifications, defended with stones by two or three dozen people; but the very fact of their being thrown up showed the revolutionary temper of the people.

Acts of terrorism, assaults on police captains and district superintendents, went on without interruption all day long. I met two comrades who told me that two hours before they had killed the assistant police captain and a district superintendent; the police were in pursuit of them, but they had managed to escape detection. After calmly telling me this, they walked away into the crowd, regardless of my urgent advice to keep out of sight for a few days, or at least to get rid of their revolvers, which would connect them with the crime. So intense was the desire of vengeance for their murdered comrades that day.

The strike had all at once assumed the proportions of a popular revolt. The temper of the people was rising, the masses were being drawn into the revolution....

But there was one thing lacking, which cooled the ardour of the crowd, and had an overwhelming effect on it. When the Cossacks rode up, presenting arms, one thought possessed the people, one cry broke from their breasts: "Weapons!" But they had none, and they ran—ran before a handful of men whom they could have overpowered with their empty hands....

At eight o'clock in the evening a comrade and I, disguised in workmen's clothes, set off to Peresyp. All was quiet now in the streets that had yesterday been watered with blood. On the way we met some workmen who were Social Democrats. They all told us that the temper of the people was despondent, that the masses were clamouring for weapons, and refusing to go into the streets unarmed.

The cry for arms rose up on all sides, and we felt that unless the Social Democrats could satisfy it, the masses would turn away from us, and the strike would be over.

Meantime news reached us of a threatening agrarian movement in the district round Odessa, and of fresh orgies of cruelty on the part of the frenzied authorities. We clenched our fists in fury; but they were empty, those strong, sinewy fists, and they dropped helplessly by our sides....

As I walked home that evening I heard, not far from the Cathedral Square, a deafening explosion. I ran in the direction of the sound, but a band of Cossacks, suddenly springing up before me, wildly brandishing their loaded whips, forced me to turn back. But from the flying crowd I learned that a bomb had been thrown at a policeman in the Cathedral Square.

The Cossacks made a frenzied rush, trampling down the crowd, and I made haste to get away from that place of danger.

What had the morrow in store for us? Every one of us fell asleep that night with that question in his mind, and no one found the real answer, no one was bold enough to imagine that a new force was coming to the aid of the revolution, that force we had felt such woeful need of during those days—that a mighty battleship, full of weapons, was at hand.

Chapter 2
The Arrival of the "Potemkin"

At ten o'clock in the morning I went out into the street, and walked towards the Nikolaevsky Boulevard.

An immense and handsome flight of steps connects the latter with the port of Odessa. The magnificent view over the open sea and the bay of Odessa makes the boulevard the favourite promenade of the aristocratic public. Elegant ladies lounge away the day in its shady avenues; rich, gaily-dressed people drive up and down with trotting thoroughbreds on the smooth asphalt road. This resort of idleness, of frivolous gaiety and mirth, forms a striking contrast to the port lying below it.

Clouds of coal-dust, the shrill whistles of tugs and the deep notes of steamer sirens, the rumble of hurrying carts, the roar of thousands of human voices, are all about us as we descend into that centre of exploited labour. Here we see not smartly dressed ladies, but barefoot men in dirt and rags; here we hear not the gay strains of the boulevard orchestra, but the unceasing roar of triumphant Capital.

That day the scene of action was to be shifted to the town itself, and all the Labour agitators had received orders to be in the central streets. I was setting off, therefore, to a Liberal of my acquaintance, with whom I had left my student's uniform overnight.

It was with no cheerful feelings that I walked through the town;

we were living through tremendous events, and we were not equal to dealing with them; the masses were ready for battle; we could not lead them, for we had no weapons. The strike could not be prolonged on pacific lines: it had reached its logical end. It had stirred and excited the whole working population of Odessa, it had aroused the peasant movement in the surrounding districts, had shaken the administrative machinery of the Odessa bureaucracy, and had led the troops to sympathize with the people. Now it must either pass into an armed insurrection or—cease.

For the former alternative arms, in small quantity at least, were essential. We had none.... And our hands dropped powerless before this blank wall.

We resolved to do our utmost that day to prolong the strike, to lead the workmen on. But to what? The whole tragedy of our position lay in the fact that we could find no answer to that question. What had we to tell the people that day? Call them on to battle? But all these days they had been giving one answer to our appeals:

"We are ready; give us arms and lead us...."

Again the same blank wall, and the movement coming up against it must stop short. I pictured to myself the depression I should find already in the ranks of my comrades, and the drooping of the warlike spirit of the previous day.

But I found no justification for my gloomy reflections in the streets; far from being deserted, the street was full of a vast, eager crowd moving rapidly in the direction in which I was going myself. The crowd grew denser and denser as I got nearer the Nikolaevsky Boulevard, and similar crowds came streaming from all the adjoining streets. That peculiar hum, always heard in a crowd that is learning of something new and unexpected, hovered over the street.

I was surprised at this excitement, but my ragged workman's clothes were likely to attract the attention of the police in that aristocratic quarter, so I did not feel free to stand still and inquire into the state of mind of the crowd. I simply quickened my pace. I soon reached my friend's house, and successfully slipping by that Russian Cerberus, the *dvornik*, I ran up the stairs to his flat. Here the inexplicable excitement of the crowd was at once explained to me.

I had scarcely got through the tedious process of changing my clothes, when my good-natured acquaintance ran in and informed me that an ironclad had steamed into the port, the crew of which had mutinied and killed their officers, and were now resolved to throw in their lot with the people.

This was such great and startling news that I did not dare believe it. I ran out into the street to convince myself of its truth.

The sea stretched in its vast immensity before me, and on its Titanic bosom proudly floated another mighty colossus—a battleship with the red flag fluttering over it.

I stood in dumb, awestruck ecstasy before this marvellous apparition. . . . But there was no standing still for long—one must hurry down to it; the work that had been begun must be finished, the great battle must be fought at last. . . . And with the joyful feeling of a soldier, who at the very moment of retreat suddenly sees powerful and unexpected reinforcements approaching, I rushed down to the port.

With me ran a crowd as joyful as I was. The farther I went the denser it became. The breath of freedom was already floating over it; it transformed men's countenances, and instead of the furious hate I had seen yesterday, an expression of clutching, trembling ecstasy was on all their faces. Shouts of "Down with Autocracy!" "Hurrah for Freedom!" rose all round, and today they were not followed by the clatter of the Cossacks' horses and the angry cries of the trampled crowd.

At last I reached a tent in which lay the body of a dead sailor. An immense crowd had gathered round it, and it was difficult to squeeze one's way through. But the masses were looking for leaders, who would tell them what to do, would give them new watchwords, and would lead them out of their uncertain position. And so as soon as they saw I was a student, they let me pass through into the tent.

In the middle of the tent lay the dead man. His face was full of a marvellous peace and radiance. On his breast was the following inscription:

> Men of Odessa! before you lies the body of Grigory Vakulintchuk, a sailor savagely killed by the senior officer of the ironclad *Prince Potemkin*, (pronounced Pahtyomkin), for saying 'The soup is not good.' Let us make the sign of the cross, and say, 'Peace to his ashes.' Let us avenge ourselves on the bloodthirsty vampires! Death to the oppressors! Death to the blood-suckers! And hurrah for freedom!
>
> Crew of the squadron flagship *Prince Potemkin*: 'One for all, all for one!'

I went out of the tent, and learned in rough outline the history of the mutiny. The crew had mutinied on account of the meat served them, had killed their officers, and come to Odessa to join the workmen. The sailors had routed the Cossacks and the police, and were now taking in coal and provisions.

A picture of our whole position rose vividly before me: the authorities amazed and thrown into confusion—the soldiers few in number, and not to be relied upon. They had already refused to fire upon the people, and would certainly not fire on the sailors. On the other side, the heightened spirit of the workmen—organisation—immense fighting forces. The sailors must at once be induced to land, to join the workmen, to take the town, and set up a republic in Odessa; then to create out of the workmen a revolutionary army, and to march on, gradually extending the field of the insurrection, and fortifying one position after another for the revolution. All haste must be made to the ironclad to begin the agitation; there was no time to wait for authorisation from the party, and I resolved to act on my own responsibility.

The workmen, to whom I said that I was a representative of the Social Democratic organisation, at once procured me a boat, and I was rowed to the ship. At the same time an immense coal-barge was towed out of the harbour by a torpedo-boat. Thousands of heads could be seen on it, and the strains of the "*Varshavianka*" floated from it. Every moment the crowd from the shore responded with a mighty "Hurrah!" A military cutter came smoothly and swiftly through the water to meet me.

"Where are you going?" they shouted to me from it.

"To the free revolutionist ship," I answered.

"And who may you be—a Social Democrat?"

"Yes."

"And what proof have you to show?"

"Social Democrats don't have passports to show; they let us go to rot in Siberia and prison without them."

"Well, get in with us."

I got into the cutter. The man who had spoken to me was Matushenko. With his short figure, his firm, vigorous features, his prominent cheek-bones and little eyes, he gave the impression of a statue cast in bronze.

"This is our chief and commander," one of the sailors said to me.

Matushenko was undoubtedly one of the leading men who took part in the *Potemkin* rising; his personality was the lever of the whole movement; and so I will ask the reader to forgive me for a brief digression, in which I will try to show this figure in its true light.

Matushenko was not a Social Democrat in the sense of one who fully comprehends and believes the tenets of Social Democracy, though he used always to call himself one. I believe, indeed, that he never was a member of the organisation, and was unacquainted with Social Democratic literature; his whole knowledge of the subject was confined to a few manifestos and pamphlets.

But nature had gifted him with power of thought, decision of character, and exceptional daring.

His superior officers, even, had always been impressed by his resourcefulness, his quickness and deftness in carrying out instructions. He was considered the best of the sailors, and had been promoted to be a chief petty officer.

He was endowed by nature with an intuitive instinct, too; he had a wonderful power of divining the mood of the mass.

But he was not a leader; he was a son of the mass, and he was only the first among them. When the crowd was silent, he was silent; when they began to awaken, he was the first to snatch up a weapon, the first to shout "Down with the oppressors!" Brave as a lion when the crowd was strong, he was at a loss and was the first to lead the retreat when the crowd ceased to feel its strength. Cruel when the crowd was full of hate, he impressed all by his gentleness when the crowd was forgiving; full of boiling energy when the temper of the crowd was rising, he sank into apathy as soon as it dropped. And his thought moved in advance of the people, but never got beyond the circle of the prejudices that hem them in.

He could not understand the position, and, relying on the strength of it, force the crowd to follow him. But he had a rare intuition, and instinctively felt not only the ruling temper of the crowd, but also what was brooding within it, and he acted in accordance with that. And so, it seemed as though he were leading it when he was following it, and that he was rousing the multitude when he was being roused with it.

He knew the people, knew their psychology, and therein lay his power and his influence. He was the foremost of them. . . .

We had scarcely got under way again when one of the sailors noticed a boat not far off with two students in it. The cutter turned its course to meet it.

"Are they your folk?" the sailors asked me.

There were two Social Democrats of my acquaintance in the boat, members of the local group of the Minority section.

★★★★★★

The Russian Social Democrat party is divided into two sections—the Majority and the Minority. The original cause of the division was difference of opinion as to the degree of centralisation necessary and practicable in the organisation of the party.

★★★★★★

I was inexpressibly delighted to see them, as it was so much easier to act, the three of us together; and we could judge better, too, of the position. So, I hastened to tell the sailors that these were comrades, and after a brief exchange of greetings they, too, were taken up by the cutter.

Swift as an arrow the cutter bore us to the gigantic ship. It got nearer and nearer to us, and at last we mounted the ladder and were on board.

Here it was at once apparent that the position was by no means so propitious as we had supposed, that we should need to make great efforts before we could succeed in inducing the sailors to go ashore. Instead of the enthusiasm we expected, we met with a lukewarm reception, and found vacillation and uncertainty. The sailors seemed, as it were, bewildered at their own action; they could not yet accustom themselves to the novelty of their new position, did not know what to do and where to go. Their one firm and definite determination was opposed to our plan. It was not to leave the ship under any circumstances, and not to take any decisive action before the arrival of the whole squadron.

From the Social Democratic organisation, they desired nothing but moral support, and the dispatch of a delegate to Sevastopol to make known what had happened to the whole fleet.

We were taken to the admiral's stateroom, where all the members of the Committee were assembled. Only there a clear account of the actual mutiny was given us, and it became obvious to us that the sailors of the *Potemkin* were a crowd of men very far indeed from possessing real revolutionary convictions. We had to proceed cautiously, not to set them against us at once.

Comrade B. addressed them first. His speech was short; but there was such force and fire in it that the temper of the sailors at once changed, and several of them began to come over to our side. Then Comrade B. informed them that he was returning to the town to lay all the facts before the organisations, and left the ship, promising the sailors to come back. Unhappily he was unable to keep this promise, as he was detained for the time by another important affair.

I was left now with Comrade Z. in the admiral's stateroom.

It was impossible to carry on propaganda among the crew at the moment, as all were occupied in loading coal; many of the committee went away to various duties, and we were condemned to a brief inactivity.

I will take advantage of this interval to describe what had happened in the ship before my arrival.

Chapter 3
The Causes of the Mutiny

Revolutionary agitation and propaganda were set afoot in the Black Sea Fleet as long ago as 1903. "Circles"' were organised among the sailors in that year, and the dissemination of leaflets had begun. And this agitation had taken a firm hold on the mass of the sailors, a process greatly assisted by the intolerable conditions in which they found themselves.

Everyone is familiar with the hideousness of the soldier's life in barracks. The same barbarous treatment, the same senseless drill, the same thieving on the part of the officers, prevail in an even grimmer form among the sailors. In the navy the dishonesty of the officers went to monstrous and ridiculous extremes. Thus, for instance, the sailors are supposed to be provided with biscuit and *galettes* during the voyage. (Biscuit consists of black bread sliced and dried, *galettes* are cakes or rolls of white bread.) As the latter are more expensive than the biscuit, the sailors were served at first rations of biscuit only; meanwhile the *galettes* went mouldy, and by the time the store of biscuit was exhausted, the sailors had to eat maggoty *galettes*.

The exploitation of the sailors became more scandalous than ever after the appointment of Tchuhnin to the command of the Fleet. This admiral invented a new means of enriching the "gallant" officers at the expense of the sailors; he gave instructions for reducing the number of free hired labourers in the government dockyards and replacing them with sailors. The money saved by this clever device of the head thief of the Black Sea Fleet went into the pockets of the good Christian officers.

All these corrupt practices were at the expense of the men who make up the more educated branch of the Russian service. The fact is that service in the fleet requires a higher degree of intelligence and understanding than service in the army. The management of the complicated weapons of naval warfare, the care of the machinery of the vessels, the signalling and wireless telegraphy, all require men of developed intelligence and of some education, and consequently the better educated of the proletariat and peasantry are drafted into the navy. It is easy to understand that such men would feel more keenly the fearful abuses of their life on board.

The life of a sailor of the Black Sea Fleet may be briefly summarized thus. At home in his village he has been oppressed by the landowner and the district commander (*zemsky natchalnik*); under the aegis of the autocracy, they have sucked his blood, and robbed him to the last crust of bread won by the sweat of his brow. Then, in the name of the *Tsar*, he has been clapped in prison, and beaten with rods for the slightest protest against the wanton tyranny of those in authority over him.

Finally, in the name of the same *Tsar*, he is dragged off to barracks, where the same noble gentlemen and pillars of the Fatherland rob him in the most shameless fashion, and trample his dignity underfoot.

And so long as he is in darkness, he bears in patience all the contumely of the *Tsar's* servants; but a blind hatred of his oppressors rankles in his heart. He hides it for the time, for he does not see his enemy clearly, and knows not how to fight him. But only let a ray of light reach him, making his position clear to him, showing him his real enemies, and putting weapons in his hands for the fight, and his uncomprehending anger will be transformed into intense and conscious hatred. The submissive slave will become a terrible avenger.

This ray of light reached the sailors by way of the Social Democratic propaganda. The most efficient agent for advertising that propaganda was Tchuhnin himself. The senseless speeches of the "hero of Otchakov" could not fail to reach all the sailors of the fleet. Over and over again he held forth upon "rioting" and the Social Democrats, abusing them mercilessly, and including all the sailors in the same category.

These sallies of the gallant admiral against the Social Democrats inevitably drew the sailors' attention to them.

"Who are these queer rioters?" the sailors wondered. "They can't be such bad fellows since our old dragon abuses them."

And the "dragon" lost no opportunity of making the sailors acquainted with them. I have already mentioned that he had instituted the employment of sailors in the government dockyards. There, working side by side with workmen who had long before been affected by the revolutionary propaganda, the sailors became familiar with the teaching of the Social Democrats, and got into touch with their organisations, and the work of conversion went on apace in the naval barracks. The disastrous war, in which the lives of sailors were senselessly thrown away by tens of thousands, and the absurd measures taken by Tchuhnin to combat the revolution, were potent allies of the Social Democrats.

In the November of 1904 the first mutiny of sailors took place. Here is a description of it given by a sailor who was an eyewitness:

> It was the 3rd of November, 1904. From the morning there had been a rumour afloat that the men were not to be allowed to pass the gates on showing the usual white tickets, but that by Tchuhnin's orders there were to be red tickets of some sort. No red tickets were issued, however. This greatly exasperated the sailors. In the evening, when the sailors returned from the Government dockyards, a crowd of some three hundred sailors gathered at the gate of the second division, and there began to be high words with the man on duty at the gate.
>
> They hissed and jeered and abused the officer on duty. Someone in the crowd threw a stone at a lamp, and there was the crash of broken glass. This served as a signal. The crowd grew more excited; shouts were heard: 'Ah, the red tickets!—we'll give you your red tickets! Beat them! Hurrah!' Stones, planks, sticks, firewood, everything they could lay their hands on, went flying at the doors and windows, at the gates and the lamps.
>
> Sailors ran out of their quarters and joined the mutineers. The noise increased. What with the shouts of 'Hurrah!' the whistling, the crash of the broken windows, the hubbub grew louder and louder. There would be a moment's hush when there were no voices to be heard. Then there would be the crash of a window, and loud battering on a door, and then again, a mighty cry: 'Hurrah!' They made their way to the officers' quarters, broke the windows, smashed up the crockery, slit open the cushions, and set fire to one part. Not one officer came forward; they all seemed to be dead. They say they hid themselves in the cellars. The sailors made their way to the marine court-martial, and broke all the windows. The bugler on duty came out, and began to sound the alarm; they snatched the bugle away from

him. In one part could be heard the sounds of the '*Marseillaise*,' where those who were organised had succeeded in collecting together. Shouts were heard: 'To the house of arrest! Set our comrades free! To the town, to the town! Take rifles and to the town!' And a tremendous hurrah was kept up continually. The whistling, battering, and shouts all made a deafening din. Then the alarm was sounded in the Brestsky infantry regiment close by. A peculiar short dry *ping* rang out somewhere near!

This was a shot fired by the future petty officers of the cruiser *Memory of Mercury*, But the tremendous threatening hurrah, the crash of broken glass, and the beating of the infantry drum did not cease. Then white lights could be seen quite close to us, and again we heard that peculiar ping! And something began to whistle with a plaintive, plaintive sound over our heads. That was the petty officers again shooting at their brother-sailors. The noise died down. Men began running away to their quarters. Here and there were shouts: 'To your rifles; we will show the damned brutes how to fire on their comrades!'

But no one heeded. Again, the peculiar dry *ping* cut through the darkness of the night, and resounded in a thousand echoes in the hills near. Someone gave a pitiful shriek. Again, they fired, and this time killed just such another miserable, broken-spirited sailor as the petty officers themselves.

The panic increased. In a short time, when all the sailors were in barracks, and there was a pretty strong patrol in the yard sent from the ships, the officers arrived on the scene. They did look such paltry, pitiful figures, it was simply sickening to look at them! Midshipman Vysokosov, commander of the 4th Company, came up to us, and began: 'Brothers! what are you doing? The time is such now that your little father, the *Tsar*, your little mother, the *Tsaritsa*, and I myself, weep, while you' . . . 'Get away, bloodsucker!' someone shouted at him. There was anger in every face, and the midshipman went away. In the yard someone treated him to a stone in the ribs. The sound of breaking windows was heard up to eleven o'clock; now one of the patrol would fling a stone at one on the sly, and now a bit of wood would be thrown from within the barracks. Every now and then a shot was fired, probably by way of warning.

Next day they went to look at the work of their hands. Fragments of tables, window-frames, broken glass, and feathers from the officers' pillows were lying about everywhere. In the men's quarters there was scarcely a pane unbroken. The officers' quarters and the court-house were an awful spectacle. In some of the officers' quarters the window-panes had been completely knocked out, and there were only the curtains left, fluttering in a desolate way. Into other window-panes stones had fallen of a *pood's* weight. (1 *pood* = about 16kg or 36lb.) In the court-house there wasn't a window unbroken. The gates were smashed up, and the gate-posts too. It all looked as though it had gone through a fierce bombardment. . . . A few days later the supposed ringleaders were arrested; then came their trial, and in the end hard labour and service in disciplinary companies.—(*Social Democrat*, No. 13: *Revolutionary Work in the Black Sea Fleet*; recollections of a former sailor, chap. vi.)

This first mass movement, aimless and unpremeditated as it was, was of great importance, because it showed the sailors the possibility of protest. Then came January 9, the rumour of which reached even the sailors' ears. The work of revolutionary propaganda gained strength; the organisation of sailors spread wider and wider, and at last organised groups of sailors had been successfully formed on almost every ship.

As the waves of the revolutionary upheaval began to rise higher and higher, and a menacing agrarian movement was stirring among the masses of the peasantry, the idea of a mutiny of the whole Fleet inevitably arose among these groups. While among the immense land forces scattered all over Russia, *Tsarism* could always reckon on finding some loyal regiments, and on crushing any mutiny among the soldiers by means of them, the success of a rising among the sailors would depend on the behaviour of a comparatively small part of the forces of Russia—namely, on the Black Sea Fleet. Every mutinous man-of-war would be a powerful fortress, with an immense store of war materials. No land forces could deal with it; it could only be subdued by the aid of similar sea Titans manned by loyal sailors.

But the sailors, quartered all together in one town and in daily contact with each other, could not fail to be aware that all their comrades were dissatisfied, that all their comrades would be in sympathy with a mutiny, that not a single ship would act against the mutineers. And so, it was psychologically natural that with the temper of opposition prevailing in the Sevastopol barracks, the sailors could take the step which it was such tedious and uphill work to induce soldiers to venture upon.

The comrades—*i.e.*, the Social Democrats—of Sevastopol were fully alive to the special nature of the position. They knew that by taking decisive steps simultaneously on all the ships they could easily bring about a general rising. And they made their plan of the mutiny accordingly.

It was to have broken out on Tendro, an uninhabited island, which the squadron visited every year for the manoeuvres. At night, at an hour fixed beforehand, those who were in the plot were to fall on the sleeping officers, bind them, tear off their epaulettes, and proclaim a republic. When the petty monarchs of yesterday were grovelling, humbled in the dust, and the sailors saw how easy it was to settle accounts with the men who had so long kept them in awe, their rankling resentment would break out; they would all join the mutiny, and the immense forces of the squadron would be in the hands of the revolutionists.

The chief obstacle to the accomplishment of this plan was the *Potemkin*. There had been scarcely any revolutionary agitation on that ship; its crew was considered the most backward of all, and it was the most powerful ironclad of the Black Sea Fleet, and might ruin the success of the whole enterprise.

But the idea of mutiny began to gain ground even there. A few days before setting out to sea, the Sevastopol committee of the Social Democratic party received a letter from the crew of the *Potemkin*, inquiring if it would do harm to the revolution if they were to mutiny. Being anxious to secure the common action of all the sailors, the committee begged the men of the *Potemkin* to take no steps before the other ironclads took action. The *Potemkin* men agreed to this.

The *Potemkin* left the harbour. . . . The composition of its crew was not particularly favourable for a mutiny; almost half the crew consisted of raw hands enrolled during the previous year. They had only just come from their villages, where the agrarian movement had not yet commenced; the terrible discipline had stupefied them and broken them in, while the propaganda of the barracks had not yet got a hold on them, and the systematic abuses of the barrack system had not yet aroused in them the same dumb hatred for the officers as in the older sailors. At the same time, they had not yet the dash and contempt for death characteristic of the hardened sailor. Half of the remainder of the crew, too, consisted of men enrolled in recent years, and only a small group of about a hundred consisted of old sailors. This group was the most determined part of the crew; from it came the members of the "committee" and all the leaders of the mutiny. And so, the sailors of the *Potemkin* were very far from being the centre of the revolutionary movement in the Black Sea. And that very fact gives the mutiny of the *Potemkin* all the more significance.

The *Potemkin* steamed out of harbour. . . . The crew had heard something of a mutiny of the fleet; there were vague exciting rumours among the sailors; they talked of Social Democrat manifestos and speeches, recalled fine sayings of a heavenly kingdom of freedom and labour. They even spoke, too, of life in the village, a life full of sorrow, privation, and hardship; thought of those who made their lives such an insufferable burden, thought, too, of the barracks and of the officers, the noble parasites, as a vicious brood preying upon them here even as in the village. They talked, too, of the thousands of workmen slaughtered in St. Petersburg, and listened to the tales of the sailors, the heroes of Tchemulpo. who were now, like themselves, beaten and robbed by the very officers who had sent hundreds of their comrades to the bottom of the sea.

They listened and brooded on these things. In the fearful heat they spend the livelong day in stupid drill of no use to anyone. . . . News reaches them from Odessa that the workmen and the peasants have risen, and are in conflict with the servants of the *Tsar*, that they are being worsted in the struggle, and are cursing their own brothers in soldiers' jackets. Their hearts are stirred, and their minds work faster; their discipline seems more senseless, their bondage more terrible. Again, rumours come of preparations for a mutiny of the sailors. But their broken spirits dare not yet cross that dread line, dare not turn on their oppressors the guns, hitherto aimed by those very officers at the people's heart. A shock was needed; a challenge from their tyrants. A bold step must be taken by one of the mass, and the rest would not be slow to follow it.

Meat was served them, meat for weary men exhausted by toil. It was full of maggots, and a sickening stench rose from it. (The writer saw the remains of this putrid meat when he visited the ironclad.) A murmur of indignation was heard among the hitherto submissive slaves; it reached the ears of their rulers, unaccustomed to reckon with the sailors' wishes.

The ship doctor inspects the meat and pronounces it of excellent quality. The commander gives the order to prepare a *borshtch* of the maggoty and stinking meat. Blinded by the power of the bayonet, he does not see in his madness that he is standing on a volcano—on the eve of an eruption.

The bell sounded for dinner.... In silence the sailors sat down in their places, took each a piece of bread and ate it, sipping water. No demands, no protests.... But accustomed to the boundless insolence of power, used all their lives to trampling the sailors' dignity under their feet, their oppressors could not tolerate even this silent protest.

The sailors are summoned by the drum to the quarter-deck; they are quickly assembled, drawn up in ranks. The captain stations himself on the capstan, and makes a speech to the men.

Do you know what is the punishment for mutiny on board a man-of-war. Do you see this mast? You will all hang on it. So don't you mutiny, but eat your *borshtch*; those willing to eat the *borshtch* cross over to the right!

But only twelve men obeyed this order; the rest stood mute. Not a sound was heard in the crowd; but their eyes gleamed with rage. And the "old wolf" was afraid. The order to fire was ready to burst angrily from his lips, but it did not come.

"Very well," he said, "if you won't eat your *borshtch* you needn't. I'll seal it up in a bottle, and lay the matter before the commander-in-chief; let him judge." With these words the captain got down from the capstan, and gave the order for the crew to disperse.

But here another tyrant, the senior officer Gilyarovsky, came forward.

"Stay," he shouted as the crew were beginning to move off. "Boatswain, call the sentry up."

A whistle was heard, followed by the hurried patter of sailors' feet, and in a minute the sentry stood facing the unarmed crew. At the sight of the loaded rifles, and the glittering bayonets the hearts of the boldest quailed.

"Those who are willing to eat the *borshtch*—to the right!" Gilyarovsky's voice rang out imperiously in the stillness. The foremost row faltered . . . and crossed over; the second row followed, and soon all the crew were moving across.

Gilyarovsky triumphed, but this was not enough for the bully; he wanted once for all to beat out of the "cattle" all desire to show themselves men. Suddenly jumping down from the capstan, he rushed at the crew and barred the way for the remaining thirty of the sailors.

"Stay! These don't want to eat the *borshtch*. Boatswain, the tarpaulin; and you can go," he added, turning to the crew. But the sailors stood without stirring, their faces white, their eyes staring with horror at the comrades who were in another instant to be shot like sheep. The sound of weeping and a smothered sob could be heard. But, blinded by terror, they did not dare lift a hand against their murderers.

"Well, why don't you go, dogs?" Gilyarovsky shouted again.

The tarpaulin was brought; and the sailors were covered with it.

"Sentry, fire!"

All was stillness, and expectation of something awful. But the sentry stood motionless.

"A mutiny!" shouted Gilyarovsky. "Wait, I'll teach you to mutiny!"

With these words he rushed at the nearest sentry and snatched his rifle from him.

"Lads, take the rifles; why are we standing looking at the damned brutes?" rang out at the same instant in the crowd of sailors.

The majority was only waiting for the signal; a sort of shock passed over it; it heaved, and with a yell rushed to the gun-deck for the rifles.

A moment later the ship was not to be recognised.

The sailors were running, and bustling to and fro. Shouts of "Hurrah! down with autocracy!" "Beat the bloodsuckers!" echoed from the batteries; in parts of the ship there was firing. There was silence only in the quarter-deck, where five or six officers stood with pale faces, hardly able to grasp what had happened. The first of the sailors to run down from the gun-deck were Matushenko and Vakulintchuk.

The former ran after Lieutenant Neupokoev, firing at him as he ran away. The second rushed without a rifle at Gilyarovsky, who was aiming at the sailors. Trying to save his comrades, he clutched the rifle by the muzzle and struggled to tear it out of Gilyarovsky's hands. The latter fired, and Vakulintchuk fell backwards at the very instant that he wrenched the rifle out of his adversary's hands. At the same instant Matushenko ran up and wounded Gilyarovsky by a shot from his rifle. The latter staggered back and fell into the water. But in his frenzy, he did not grasp his position, even as he fell.

"I'll give it to you!" he shouted to Matushenko; "I'll teach you to mutiny . . . I know you! . . ."

Horror and excitement reigned supreme in the ship. Shouts of "Down with autocracy!" and "Hurrah!" mingled with the shots fired by the sailors and the cries of the officers. Many of the latter threw themselves in the water, and the sailors fired on them there.

Captain Golikov ran out on to the deck with nothing but his shirt on, meaning to jump into the sea and swim to the torpedo-boat. At the sight of the sailors he threw himself on his knees and humbly begged for mercy. But he had ill-treated the sailors too long; they had suffered too much at his hands; their outraged dignity craved vengeance for all their humiliations, and Golikov fell a victim of the popular fury.

All of a sudden someone shouted that one of the officers had run down to the mine apparatus to blow up the ironclad. A fearful panic took possession of the sailors. Many of them jumped straight into the water in the face of the firing at the officers. The most determined of them ran to the mining department and dragged out Lieutenant Ton.

"If you care to join us, take off your epaulettes," Matushenko said to him.

"Fool, it was not you gave them me, and you shall not take them away," he answered, and fired his revolver at Matushenko.

The bullet flew by him, and at the same instant Matushenko shot him dead. He was the only officer who knew how to face death for his honour.

Meanwhile some of the officers had swum to the torpedo-boat, and the latter began all at once to manoeuvre in a strange way. Again, there was panic on the ironclad, the sailors shouting that the torpedo-boat was going to blow up the ship. A huge gun was loaded at once and aimed at the torpedo-boat. But the men in the boat signalled that there was no mine on board, and so saved it. And they arrested the officers there and brought them to the ship.

Already voices had been raised in protest against further slaughter. The first fearful outburst was over, the pent-up hatred of long years had found a vent, and now someone shouted: "Enough killing; don't let them say we are like our 'Herods.'" All the sailors responded to this appeal.

They began to seek out the officers, who had hidden themselves in various corners of the ship. The priest was hauled out from some hiding-place. This reverend gentleman was never seen sober, but the flush of drink had left his face, and his eyes strayed about in a scared way, as he humbly muttered something about his sympathy with the sailors. He was placed under arrest in the wardroom.

Dr. Smirnoff was found wounded by a bullet; he was almost breathing his last, and begged the sailors to let him die in peace....

His corpse was thrown into the sea.

On the shield, (an iron support, serving as a rest for aiming the big guns during manoeuvres), they found Engineer Kovalenko, Midshipman Kaluzhny, and another officer. Several officers were found in the admiral's stateroom.

All were stripped of their epaulettes, put in the wardroom, and a guard was set over them.

The lieutenant, Alexeieff, too, made his appearance.

"Don't kill me; I was always on your side," he said to the crew. He really had always behaved decently to the sailors, and the latter contented themselves with cutting off his epaulettes.

At last they had completed the destruction of the old order of things. Now they had to create new methods, a new organisation. They set the ship to rights and called the crew together.

Free speeches were for the first time uttered on this ship, where, till then, nothing had been heard but the coarse abuse of the officers and the smothered curses of the downtrodden sailors. They spoke of the struggle for freedom, of the mutiny being supported by all the squadron, of the rising in Odessa, of the necessity of going there to join the squadron. But till the squadron appeared, all the sailors would remain on the ship, which was a stronghold and refuge for them. And first of all, they must elect a committee of control, not such rulers as had tortured and insulted the sailors, but leaders from among the comrades they loved and trusted. There must be order and discipline on the ironclad, maintained by willing agreement and love for their work.

They elected thirty sailors to form a committee of control.

This committee superintended all the sailors' duties, had complete control of the funds of the ship, and was empowered to give orders for arrest, and to open negotiations with the authorities and with organisations (*i.e.*, revolutionary societies). In fact, it might have become an absolutely sovereign power in the ship. But it did not actually become so; it was only during the first few days that it settled every question on its own responsibility. Later on, its influence was sensibly weaker. Even in the brief period of its greatest authority it did not decide on the most important actions, but submitted them to the consideration of the whole crew. In the later days meetings of the whole crew became more and more frequent.

In doing this the committee argued quite justly: "If we want the majority to stand firm, to take an intelligent moral view of their duties, they must be drawn into the sphere of the whole life of the ship;

we must bring out their independence, and train them to think of the necessity of standing up for themselves and being their own masters."

For the same reason, the sittings of the committee were public, and from one to two hundred men were always present at them, and were not merely passive spectators, but expressed their approval and disapproval of the speeches, delivered their opinions, and almost always voted.

And so, the real control of the ship did not lie in the committee, but in a large part—the more intelligent part—of the crew.

The navigation of the ship they entrusted to the navigating lieutenant, Alexeieff, and the boatswain, Murzak. The former they appointed captain, the latter, senior officer.

In their first steps in revolution the unreflecting are always guided by two impulses, the revolutionary instinct, and the habit of the old traditions. The former impels them to break with the past and to create new institutions, but a tribute has to be paid to the latter also. History furnishes many examples of this.

The *Potemkin* was no exception in this respect; and the crew, though they created a new revolutionary institution—the committee—yet paid their tribute to the old traditions, which told them that a vessel must be commanded by an officer, and so the sailors appointed an insignificant man, Alexeieff, as their captain.

I say this in defiance of the opinion that this course was inevitable, that no one but Alexeieff was capable of navigating the ship. This is contradicted by the facts: the ironclad was always navigated, not by Alexeieff, but by the sailors. Alexeieff hardly superintended them at all, and if he did take any command on himself, it was simply to introduce confusion and disorganisation into the sailors actions.

He was a worthless creature. . . . Terrified that he would be killed, he tried to convince the sailors that he had always been on their side, and from the same terror he undertook the command of the ship. But when he had taken that step, he began to be terrified by another danger—the punishment awaiting him from the authorities. And then he began to meditate turning traitor to the crew, but being a poor creature, he could not bring himself to act openly and on his own account. He acted stealthily and through others.

When the question was discussed whether to fire on the town or not, he did not let drop a single word, in spite of repeated requests from the sailors for his opinion. But once in a moment of consternation he uttered the treacherous word: "Roumania. . . ." Though he was afraid of taking command of the vessel, he did not dare to refuse openly to do so, but pretended to be ill. But at the moment when the squadron was approaching, he took the command in the hope of betraying us.

He was not an out-and-out traitor (of the class of Dr. Golenko), remaining on the ship simply in order to betray it. He was a man of too little character for that. But he was a traitor by circumstance; he acted treacherously to save his paltry life. And if history had not played such a prank on him, making him the leader of a mutiny, he might have been an honest man. When one thinks of his petty character, one instinctively recalls those immortal words of Zola's: "What scoundrels these honest people are!"

Such was the feeble being into whose hands the sailors put authority. They felt it necessary that authority should be in the hands of an officer—that a man of that class should be leader over them. They hated, "the skin!"—as the sailors call the officers—but still their prestige was great over them.

Prejudices absorbed by long years of barrack discipline are not easily broken down; they retain a mysterious influence over a mass of men even when all have individually revolted against them.

Alexeieff and Murzak were to report their actions to the committee, and to carry out the instructions of the latter. In reality, such reports were not made. The majority of the sailors, ignorant and unreflecting, did not demand them, and we could not look after everything. This was, of course, a great omission on our part, as, by exposing the doings of our officers, we could have shown the crew their unfitness to lead the mutiny. Though they followed the instructions of the committee in the details of everyday life, these gentlemen proved to be extraordinarily inert and irresolute in the most critical moments, and thus caused terrible disorganisation in the ranks of the sailors.

And the whole issue of the mutiny depended on such decisive moments. To minimise this weakness in our organisation, I proposed that an executive sub-committee should be elected from the committee, to be associated with our officers in the executive control. We put into this sub-committee the men most devoted to the revolution. But they were devoid of initiative, and the control still remained in feeble hands. To be victorious we should have had a strong leader—a man of resolution, and experienced in naval matters....

There was no such man....

When they had at last completed the organisation of the new

management of the ship, the sailors determined to set off for Odessa, to the defence of the people in revolution there. To be accurate, they had no clear notion why they were going to Odessa, and what they would find there. Unconsciously they went there in obedience to the revolutionary instinct, which told them that there the people were in revolt, and would give them help. It was this same instinct which made them hold their heads higher, as soon as they heard of the rising in Odessa.

While the sailors were busy with these matters, in the ship's infirmary there lay quietly dying the first victim of the sailors' revolt, Vakulintchuk, paying with his life for the deliverance of his comrades. He lay unconscious, hearing none of those words of freedom on the ship of which he had dreamed all the long years of his service at sea. The sailors crowded round him; some of them could not control their tears: they wept like children, these rough men, hardened by suffering. Only for a minute before his death Vakulintchuk came to himself. "Well, how is it with the ship?" was his first question.

"We have avenged you, dear comrade; we have done for the officers, and now we have freedom," answered a sailor, standing by him.

"Good! good!" Vakulintchuk murmured faintly, and his face lighted up with joy.

He tried to say something more, but Death held him tight in his chill embrace, and a moment later he breathed his last.

So died that hero, who in his death taught the sailors that motto of the proletariat, which they put in their appeal to the inhabitants of Odessa:

All for one and one for all.

Meanwhile the ship was making at full speed towards Odessa, and at ten o'clock in the evening the *Potemkin* cast anchor at the entrance to the bay of Odessa.

The committee assembled in the admiral's stateroom. The sailors had a feeling of self-satisfaction, as they sat on the soft sofas. One of them lolled in a low chair and smoked a cigar. Jokes and witticisms were interchanged. But they were soon over, for their position called for serious consideration; they had to deliberate on their further course of action.

After long discussion they came to the following resolutions: (1) Early next morning to send the "leaders of the *artels*" to the town to purchase provisions; (2) to obtain the necessary supply of coal; (3) to carry the body of Vakulintchuk on shore with an inscription appealing to the people; (4) to write out a detailed account of what had taken place at Tendro, and to examine all the officers; (5) to address appeals to the people of the town of Odessa, to the Cossacks, and to the French Consul; (6) to get into touch with all the Social Democratic organisations.

✶✶✶✶✶✶

Artels are groups or gangs. Russians, when engaged in any common pursuit or industry, habitually form themselves into *artels*, each with a leader, for messing together and common action of all kinds.

✶✶✶✶✶✶

They counted over the ship's purse also, and found there twenty-four thousand *roubles*. The composition of the detailed report and of the appeals was entrusted to one of the sailors. Here is a copy of one of them:

> From the crew of the *Prince Potemkin Tavritchesky*.
> We beg all the Cossacks and the army immediately to lay down their arms, and to unite all together in the struggle for freedom. The last hour of our suffering has come; down with the autocracy! We have freedom already; we are already acting independently, without government over us. Government is abolished. If there shall be resistance offered us, we beg peaceable citizens to get out of the town. In case of resistance the town will be destroyed.

Later in the day, after there had been aggressive action on the part of the police, the sailors composed a second manifesto addressed to the French Consul. I append a copy of this second appeal:

> To the French Consul,
> To His Excellency the French Consul. From the ironclad *Prince Potemkin Tavritchesky*,
> Most honoured public of the town of Odessa—By the crew of the ironclad *Prince Potemkin Tavritchesky* there was brought today, the 15th of June, from the ship a dead body which was placed at the disposal of the workmen's party for interment with the usual ceremony. Sometime afterwards a sloop was sent by those workmen to the ship, which informed them that the guard set over the dead body had been driven away by the Cossacks. The body was left without anyone in charge. The crew of

the ironclad begs the public of Odessa (1) not to offer hindrance to the burial of the sailor from the ship; (2) to watch vigilantly that it may take place with all due ceremony; (3) to pray the police and also the Cossacks to cease their vain onslaught, because this is altogether useless; (4) not to prevent the workmen's party from procuring the goods necessary for the crew of the ironclad; (5) the crew begs the public of Odessa to comply with all the above enumerated requests. In case of refusal in all the above matters, the crew will have to resort to the following measures: There will be a bombardment of the town from all the guns. Wherefore the crew forewarn the public, and in case of firing arising, they beg those who do not desire to take part in the resistance to withdraw from the town. Moreover, we are expecting assistance from Sevastopol—several ironclads for this purpose—and then it will be worse.

In their simplicity, the sailors imagined that the representative of free France would extend his powerful protection to a movement for freedom anywhere, and so they decided that this appeal, intended for the people of Odessa, should be presented to the French Consul for publication by him.

It was close upon dawn when the sitting of the committee was over; but they had no thought of sleep. They set to work to carry out all their resolutions.

Three sailors went ashore and entered the town.

It was silent and deserted in the slumbering streets. Nothing but the tram-cars lying on their sides and the patrol of Cossacks recalled the stormy scenes of the previous day.

The sailors reached the shops that always furnished provisions for the fleet, meeting with no hindrance, as no one in the town was yet aware of the mutiny on the *Potemkin*. The shopkeepers promptly dispatched the goods they ordered to the port, and at seven o'clock, with the help of some workmen, to whom the matter was explained, they had conveyed everything to the ship.

Meanwhile, Vakulintchuk's body was dressed in clean clothes, and the inscription I have transcribed already was hung on his breast.

By this time, it was possible to act openly, and Vakulintchuk's body was carried on shore. It was laid out in the harbour, and several sailors armed with rifles remained to guard it. The people crowded round it, and the sailors told them all that had happened.

The workmen were filled with indescribable enthusiasm. Loud shouts of "Hurrah!" welcomed the cutters from the ship as they approached the harbour. A tent was put up over the corpse, and a cup set beside it. The people flung their money liberally into the cup to subscribe for a monument to the hero.

Hearing that the sailors needed coal, the workmen seized a steamer loaded with coal and proceeded to tow it by a torpedo-boat to the ship.

It was at that moment that I ran down to the harbour and set off to the ship.

The mutiny on the *Potemkin* was not simply a mutiny on account of putrid meat, as our "patriotic" newspapers have zealously tried to prove. The underlying causes of it were deeper and more serious. They must be looked for in the fearful disorder of our life, and in the revolutionary movement which is gaining a hold on all Russia. It was only this which gave strength and power to an ignorant body of men to accomplish this splendid deed. Had there been no atmosphere of revolution, there would have been no *Potemkin*; there would have been nothing but an obscure ironclad of no interest to anyone, the *Prince Potemkin Tavritchesky*.

Chapter 4

The First Day

I did not stay long in the admiral's stateroom; I soon came out on to the quarter-deck. Again, a magnificent scene lay stretched before my eyes.

The bay, covered with a perfect forest of masts of gigantic steamers, was dotted now with sloops. Revolutionary songs came floating from them, and red flags fluttered over them. Thousands of workmen were bringing tobacco, sugar, and tea to the ironclad.

It was touching to see these men—famished by a whole month's strike—spending their last mites on "presents" for their brothers the sailors. The sloops came alongside, left their offerings, and rowed off again in the midst of loud greetings from the sailors. Fresh and fresh ones kept coming to take their place. The men were laughing with glee, and the sea and the sun and all nature was laughing with them.

Never shall I forget that marvellous spectacle of the people fraternizing with their sons who had returned to them. While I stood fascinated, gazing at this picture, Dymtchenko, one of the sailors most devoted to the revolution, came up to me. He was the captain of the watch for that day.

His sunburnt, irregular, but wonderfully soft features, and his naive, childlike eyes, attracted everyone at once. Full of faith in men and simplehearted courage, he was like a grown-up child. Even now I recall with a warm feeling his cordial voice as he said: "Here, comrades, a good man wants to say a word to you; come, then, let us hear him." He was ready to go through fire for that "good man," ready any moment to lay down his life for the common cause. But this manly fellow was without initiative, and lost his head at moments of emergency. He lost his head from the sense of the immense responsibility laid upon him; from the knowledge that the life of others depended on what he did. And then he was incapable of prompt decisive action. He could not be a leader, but life had fastened the burden of that position on him.

Dymtchenko informed me that two gentlemen were on the ironclad, calling themselves members of the Social Democratic organisation, and begged me to identify them. I found them to be Kirill and another comrade, a member of the Bund.

Kirill, with his tall figure, blunt features, and fair, bushy beard, looked like a typical peasant of Great Russia. His appearance always made an immediate impression on simple workpeople.

"That's a peasant of the real sort; we must listen to him, brothers," was always said of him by the very workmen who before his arrival had been unwilling to listen to Social Democratic speakers. And the peasant "of the real sort" would begin speaking in a mighty voice, developing before his audience the Social Democratic programme.

His arrival on the ship was very fortunate, for Dymtchenko at once proposed to call a mass meeting of sailors. We agreed to this, of course, and were soon standing in the forecastle surrounded by hundreds of sailors.

I was the first speaker. I described to the sailors the leading points in the present position of the workers, told them of the struggle of the proletariat, and urged on the sailors that they should rally round the watchword for which the workers in St. Petersburg were dying in thousands—"Death or freedom." The sailors echoed this watchword in a thunder of voices, and it was carried far, far out over the world, telling it of the new depth of the Russian revolution—of the beginning of the end.

The enthusiasm was growing.

Then our comrade, the Bundist, began to speak. He spoke of brotherhood and equality, of the solidarity of the proletariat, of the

Social Democratic party marching at the head of the working class.

"And hand in hand with the proletariat of all lands," he concluded, "you, sailors, their brothers, give a mighty cheer: Hurrah for socialism! Hurrah for freedom!"

Again, the tremendous "Hurrah!"

The sailors listened, all eagerness and impatience; they were longing to hear again fiery words of freedom.

Kirill got up; but at that moment the bell rang for dinner, and the sailors invited us to join them. We were glad to accept their invitation, for we had eaten nothing all the morning. Surrounded by a dense crowd of sailors, we went below. We were offered a little glass of vodka; then we were seated on long benches beside the sailors. The faces of all were excited. Our hearts, too, were throbbing joyfully.... "Can it be it's not a dream? Can the freedom of Russia be so near?" I longed to shake hands; I could have hugged them all in a burst of holiday feeling. And at that instant I felt someone squeeze my hand. I turned round; it was the Bundist. He, too, was feeling as I did. We stood in silence, looking into each other's eyes, and one of us murmured: "Can it be?"... That simple phrase said all. And around us all the while the gay, noisy talk of the awakening mass.

★★★★★★★★★★

After dinner it was impossible to continue our propaganda, as the task of taking in coal had to be completed, and all hands were called off to work.

We (Kirill, the Bundist, and I) went to the admiral's stateroom, where we found authorised representatives of all the Social Democratic organisations who had by now arrived on the vessel. They were deliberating with the committee on a plan of action, and I went on deck, as I was not one of the representatives.

A number of people was crowding on the ship. Some of the public were occupied in inspecting the vessel, peeping into all parts of it, jostling and hindering the sailors in their work. And a chaotic disorder prevailed in the ship from this cause.

All this, together with the novelty of their position, could not but be annoying to sailors accustomed to order and discipline, and they began to insist that all landsmen should leave the ship. Just then the committee rose from its deliberations, and the sailors' demand was laid before it. Fully grasping the justice of this demand, the comrades made no protest against it, deciding to leave only three on board to represent them—Kirill, Comrade A., and myself.

I was briefly informed of the proceedings at the recent meeting. To do our leaders justice, at this first step they made one of those blunders which they made without ceasing in the sequel—a blunder arising from lack of decision in the novel and exceptional position in which they were placed: they did not raise the question of the sailors' landing and taking the town. They did not even attempt to overcome the disinclination of the sailors to act before the arrival of the squadron.

Consequently, this difficult task lay entirely on our shoulders. We undertook it; but while doing so, we expected to be reinforced by fresh help from the town. Reckoning on receiving support in propaganda and oratory, we resolved first of all to overcome the sailors' mistrust of "freemen," as they called everyone not belonging to the crew. The reader will see later on that our expectation was not fulfilled; no comrades arrived, and the leadership of the mutiny devolved upon us entirely.

The last sloop with our comrades had at last pushed off; all the ladders had been drawn up on the ironclad, and we were cut off from the shore for the day.

Though the squadron could not be expected to arrive yet, the committee determined in any case to be prepared for its arrival. The loading of coal was over, and the order was given to clear the deck—*i.e.*, wash it and close the hatchways to all parts leading from it. The sailors were busily occupied in setting the ship to rights. I was standing on the quarter-deck, gazing at the shoals of boats covering the bay, when, happening to glance at one of them, I stared at it in astonishment. Two soldiers were in it, rowing vigorously towards the ironclad. As soon as the boat was alongside, I rushed towards it.

"What have you come here for?" I asked the soldiers.

"We are delegates from our regiments."

I ran to the sailors to tell them the news. The ladder had been put away, and a rope-ladder was let down to the soldiers.

In a moment they were standing on the quarterdeck, surrounded by sailors.

"Brothers," one of them began, in a voice breaking with emotion, "the soldiers of our two regiments—the *Ismailovsky* and the *Dunaisky*—have sent us to tell you that we are with you. You can even go into the town, brothers; no one will touch you. As soon as you step on shore, we will come over to you at once."

"And a good thing, too," said one of the sailors, "or friends would be marching against each other; it has long been high time. But one thing: we won't come ashore at once, because we are waiting for the whole squadron. You make ready meanwhile. And, mind you, don't hurt the people."

The sailors warmly seconded this speech, and the soldiers, accompanied by friendly greetings, left the ironclad, and soon disappeared beyond the waves.

The daring act of these simple men, who had ventured in soldiers' tunics to visit a mutinous ironclad, showed the temper of the army, and had an encouraging effect on the sailors. They set to their work with greater vigour and energy. Comrade A. and I went to the admiral's stateroom to deliberate on a plan of common action.

Kirill, who had had no sleep the previous night, stretched himself out in a low chair and fell asleep. We made up our minds not to disturb him, and discussed our plans without him.

A.'s ideas fully coincided with my plan—to devote all our efforts to inducing the sailors to take action against the town without waiting for the squadron. But we had to proceed with caution. It was not difficult to dispose the committee in our favour, but the crew were not so easy to deal with. We had already received an intimation of this. A comrade of the Majority group, a girl, who had been on the ironclad that day, had delivered an eloquent address, in which she besought the sailors to land. I was not present at this comrade's speech, and did not see the audience nor the impression produced on them. But one of the sailors came up to me and said:

"The young lady speaks well, only what she proposes isn't handy for us; we can't go ashore."

Meanwhile the "conductors," too, were not idle. (Sailors who remain voluntarily in the fleet after their term of compulsory service has expired.) They kept up an unceasing agitation against the "landsmen" and against politics. At the time of the mutiny they had been arrested, but afterwards, on their expressing a desire to join the rising, they were set free. This was a terrible mistake, as they formed a rallying-point for reaction. Now, their watchword was, "Away with the landsmen!" and the feeling it expressed was gaining more and more ground among the sailors. It had been greatly strengthened by the disorganisation, due to the numbers of the public visiting the ironclad, which I have referred to.

We had to beware of wasting our energies. Kirill and I had to carry on the propaganda alone, for A., owing to the weakness of his voice, could only help in deciding on our course of action. While we were talking things over together, we heard a shout: "The squadron!" We rushed on deck, and this was the scene that met our eyes: All the sailors were standing at the side of the ship with their eyes fixed on the horizon. There a curl of smoke could be seen in the distance; it came closer, and soon a vessel could be made out. It turned out to be a small naval steamer, not even provided with guns—the *Viekha*. It was resolved, however, to capture her.

The captain of this vessel, which had left Nikolaev in the morning, knew nothing of the mutiny. He came calmly towards us and saluted with his flags. The *Potemkin* replied, and signalled instructions to the *Viekha* to come alongside us on the starboard side, and to the captain to come on board and report.

The captain, suspecting nothing, carried out these instructions punctiliously, and came aboard in full dress uniform, with the ribbons of his orders on his breast. He had scarcely stepped on the ship when he was surrounded by a guard, and Matushenko, informing him that he was under arrest, asked him for his cutlass and his epaulettes. The captain was thunderstruck; amazement, terror, and wrath passed in succession over his face. He did not know whether it was the practical joke of a drunken sailor or reality.

But the determined faces of the sailors and their loaded rifles showed him that something serious had happened; and Matushenko informed him that the sailors and the people had risen against their oppressors, and that, in the name of the people, he declared him under arrest. Then at last the poor captain understood what had happened, and his face twitched with terror.

"Well, brother, I was always on your side. My men are always comfortable," he articulated, faltering with alarm.

"All right! all right! You can talk later on, but now hand over your epaulettes and your cutlass."

He was very loath to part with his epaulettes. He scanned all the faces, as though seeking some support. But he saw a malicious smile on every countenance, while Matushenko, holding a revolver, confronted him with a stern face. And the gallant warrior made haste to pull off his epaulettes. Life was dearer to him than honour.

"Now go into the admiral's stateroom. Sentry, on duty!" Matushenko commanded.

But again the captain entreated him.

"Let me go to my ship, brothers; I shan't run away from you, you know. I have a woman with a baby on board."

"Your wife?"

"No, someone else's...."

The sailors laughed in chorus.

"It's the wife and child of your Captain Golikov, brothers. Let me go to her. She must be protected from insult."

The last words made the sailors indignant.

"What, are we criminals? No fear; we're not like you. We won't touch a woman. You go along, or you see this . . .?" and with these words Matushenko, getting irritated, raised his revolver. The captain obediently trotted off to the admiral's stateroom. There a report of the proceedings was read over to him, and he had to sign it. Then one of the comrades, either Kirill or A.—I don't remember which—made a splendid speech, describing the awful condition of Russia, which drove the people, and with them the forces, to revolt.

Meanwhile signals were given from our ship to the *Viekha* that the captain desired all his officers to come on board.

The latter were not long in appearing, and they gave up their epaulettes quite as hurriedly as their captain. Not one of them attempted to protest. They were led to the admiral's stateroom, where about a hundred sailors were already assembled. As soon as they had been brought in, I made a speech, which concluded with the following words:

> At last the long looked-for day has come, when the people, driven to revolt, are arresting their oppressors and judging them for all their crimes.

These last words, taken in conjunction with the revolver which I held casually in my hands, made a powerful impression on the officers. They turned green with terror, and began to protest that they had always been on the side of the people, and were in sympathy with the struggle for freedom.

It was sickening to see those cowardly slaves, only yesterday full of arrogant pride in their noble rank and distinguished position, today ready to fall at the feet of the men they had always beaten and despised, simply to save their paltry lives.

And all our defeats in the East were explained: could officers like these lead men to victory?

Meanwhile the ship's chest of the *Viekha* had been brought on board and was being opened. The iron chest was not easy to open, and the sailors jested on this: "They have been sharp enough to build their money-chests stronger than their ironclads."

"What nonsense the silly chap's talking! Money's not like men—if you lose it, you can't find more so easily."

At last the chest was opened. There turned out to be about two thousand *roubles* in it.

Meanwhile the sailors of the *Viekha* informed us that they had nothing against their officers, and begged us not to kill them. The committee, on receiving this request, decided to send the officers ashore. The sailors showed themselves more magnanimous than their officers: they resolved to provide the latter with money, and gave them a hundred *roubles* each.

And after that the reptile press has dared to call the sailors "drunken robbers," and Madame Golikov has spoken of them as "a criminal gang of murderers"—Madame Golikov, whom the sailors resolved not to tell all at once about her husband's death for fear of overwhelming her with the shock. Their rough hearts, little used to delicacies of feeling, prompted them to respect sorrow even in a person so near the hated tyrant, who had not thought twice about shooting at sailors for being unwilling to eat putrid meat. But that pampered fine lady did not scruple to give vent to unseemly abuse and slander of sailors, when they were arrested and facing death! Public opinion will judge between her and them. . . .

At last they had done with the officers and taken them ashore. The first arrest of a vessel of the *Tsar* was completed. It was a great moment—the first step in the extension of the revolt; already we seemed to see the whole fleet with red flags fluttering over every ship.

This incident had a specially happy effect on the sailors, who were building great hopes on the support of the whole squadron.

****

Evening had fallen over the sea before all the work had been done, and we could arrange a meeting. The crew assembled on the gun-deck and A. and I went there. In the covered place near the kitchen and machinery, with seven hundred sailors crowding in it, it was close and hot. The sailors formed an amphitheatre, the front rows sitting down, the back rows standing one above another. In the centre stood Alexeieff, Dymtchenko, Matushenko, A., and I.

Alexeieff gave the crew a brief account of what he had done on the ironclad; a purely technical report was also made by one of the committee. It was our turn next, and Dymtchenko introduced us by the words, "Here are good men who want to say a word to us."

But the "conductors" were on the alert: several voices cried, "Away with landsmen!" Almost all the crew took up the cry. Dymtchenko looked at me and flung up his hands in despair. The critical moment had come; if we did not make the crew listen to us now, our game was lost. Now or never!

A. was equal to the emergency. He got up, and in a loud and distinct voice articulated:

> Sailors! You must not dare to refuse to hear us: we are not speaking for ourselves, but in the name of all the working people of Russia. You are the sons of these people, and must listen to their message. If you do not agree with us, we will go away, but hear us you must. In the name of the people we demand it!

These words made a great impression on the sailors. Many of them began to shout for hearing us; the "conductors" shouted against it. But the former gained the day, and we had to leave to speak.

I began to speak. The feeling that the fate of the revolution depended perhaps on my words gave me strength. My mind worked more quickly, and my words flowed freely. I don't remember exactly how long I spoke, I think for about two hours.

I began with the mutiny on the *Potemkin* and the life of the soldiers. I told the sailors that what was really wrong was not the soup, but all the conditions of their life; not their individual officers, but the order of things, which guaranteed officers complete impunity for acts of cruelty and tyranny. If they were to get better soup, better officers one day, the next they might be given maggots and bullets again.

What was wanted was security against capricious despotism. Under the regime of the autocracy this could never be guaranteed.

The sailors might any moment be carried off into warfare; for whose benefit? The autocracy's. And so, it was with that they had to struggle. How could it be done? Could the sailors hope to triumph over it with their forces alone? No! On whom then could they reckon? On the people, and on the people alone. Whether the squadron would join them was a question, but the people were their allies already.

I spoke of the sufferings of the workers and of the peasants; told them how those sufferings had driven the workers to go to the *Tsar*. The *Tsar* had replied with whips and bullets. It was the struggle of the whole people against the *Tsar*. The Russian people was now carrying on a terrible struggle against *Tsarism*, and this was the guarantee that they would help the sailors. To join them meant victory, without them they must be defeated. The workers of Odessa had shown only that day that they would stand by the sailors to the last drop of their blood. The sailors of the *Potemkin* were the first who dared to bridge over the separation between the people and the forces.

Let them pass boldly along that bridge, and, uniting with the people in the great conflict, conquer liberty for them.

As I spoke, the temper of the audience rose. What contributed not a little to the effect of my words was that I made my audience take part in my speech, asking them after every statement whether I spoke the truth or not.

At first, they answered uncertainly, as though afraid of agreeing with those strange "landsmen," as though fearing they might be leading them into some trap. But as I went on, they chimed in "True" more unanimously, and even interspersed remarks of their own; and the end of my speech was received with a mighty and prolonged "Hurrah!" The sailors were especially affected by the description of the 9th of January. A. told me that many of the sailors shed tears when they heard from me the details of the *Tsar's* cruel betrayal of the people's trust.

The temper of the crowd had changed for the better. Now not one traitor dared to shout "Away with the landsmen," and the sailors begged that one of us would speak again. But the stifling closeness prevented us from staying longer on the gun-deck, and it was decided that the meeting should move to the quarter-deck.

The attitude to us, too, had undergone a striking change. I had no coat on; and by now the evening was cool. One of the sailors came up to me and said that I might catch cold; several others ran for my coat. I asked for a drink, and tea was brought to me at once.

We went out on the open deck. It was a fresh, dark night; but the rays of the searchlight gaily dancing on the water lighted up the darkness.

On deck we found Kirill, come back from the *Viekha*. I told him of the sailors' request, and, taking his stand on the capstan, he began to speak. His voice rang out musically in the darkness of the night, and it seemed that it was a ray of light penetrating just such darkness enfolding those downtrodden men till that day. His speech was like a continuation of mine. He spoke of the Constituent Assembly for framing the Constitution, of the political and economic needs of the workers and of the peasants.

Their sympathy was already on our side; but yet we had a great deal of work before us. We had to familiarize the sailors more closely with our teaching. To do this we needed fresh forces. Whole days had to be spent in propaganda among the sailors, to enlighten them on the many defects of our life. We had widened the scope of our agitation; it needed to go deeper also. We had roused their spirit and their sympathy; but the sympathy evoked by our speeches should have been secured strongly on our side. But this we could not do. We were but three, and the whole leadership of the rising was laid upon us. It was not physically possible for us to do more than we did, and that was little. We expected assistance, but, as the reader will see later, it did not come.

This was a terrible blunder on the part of our Social Democrat societies.

The whistle calling the committee to the admiral's stateroom, cut short further speeches. The members of the committee filed off, and sat down on chairs at a long table; the sailors who did not belong to the committee stood up behind them.

There was a flood of free speech in that room, over the threshold of which the opposition had not till then dared to set its foot. The portraits of the *Tsars* and grand dukes looked mournfully down from the walls, recalling their better days. They were a discordant note in this hall of freedom, but all were so occupied that they did not think of smashing them or taking them down.

Alexeieff proposed that the committee should hear the three officers, who wanted to join us. This proposition led to much discussion; people interrupted one another, and did not let one another speak. A tremendous hubbub arose, and it became clear that we should arrive at no conclusion till we appointed a chairman. A. thereupon described that institution to the sailors, and they eagerly caught at the idea of electing a chairman. Comrade A. was the one elected.

Then the committee passed to the resolution to hear the officers, and soon after Dr. Golenko, Midshipman Kaluzhny, and Engineer Kovalenko were led in by an escort of armed sailors.

The first to speak was Kovalenko.

He was a man still young, with thick fair hair, and a good-humoured, mild face. More a Liberal than Revolutionist in his convictions, he was of a soft disposition, unfitted for conflict. But the great moment of the people's revolution awakened what force there was in him, and he joined the ranks of its champions.

The adherence of an officer and a genuine man to our side might have been of the greatest assistance to our cause. But, for all that, he should have been a man marked by determination and an unfaltering stability of character. He should have been a man able to go forward in face of anything; his voice should never have lost the ring of authority and determination.

These characteristics Kovalenko did not possess. There was always a certain lack of confidence in his speeches. His gentle nature could not become reconciled to the cruelties of revolution. He was ready to give his own life for the people, but to urge others to do so, not to shrink from shedding blood—that he could not do. And hence he did not give us what he might have given.

Kovalenko began by saying that he had always sympathised with the movement; that he had worked formerly in the Little Russian party, that now he was present at such a moment he would look on it as a disgrace to him to go ashore instead of remaining in the ranks of the mutineers.

There was the note of sincerity in his speech, but in it, as in all his speeches, there was none of the strength of a leader.

Golenko spoke next.

A perfectly bald, white-skinned, dapper little man, he looked like a typical, pampered little nobleman.

Though his speech was similar in its general tenor to Kovalenko's, it had none of the diffidence that marked the latter—nor, indeed, of the sincerity. There was a certain tone of self-complacency in it, and here and there an attempt to flatter the sailors. Still, it was impossible from it to detect in him the future agent provocateur.

Kaluzhny, the midshipman, a sickly-looking, undersized lad, only said a few words of his desire to join us.

I have often wondered what it was that induced him to take that step.

During the whole time he lay on the sofa in the wardroom, and never stirred except to get up in order to swallow a scanty dinner. His eyes strayed listlessly about the room all the while, and there was something dull and crushed about the whole of his little figure. It was clearly not from a passion for freedom that he remained on board.

I never once, even at the most successful moments of the rising, saw a gleam of pleasure in his dull eyes. But it was no desire to betray us either that induced him to remain in the ship; spending the whole day full length on the sofa, and taking no part in the life of the ship, he could not have contrived us any harm.

It was only later on in prison that I learned from the "investigating magistrate" the secret springs of his action. He fancied that the town was in the hands of the revolutionists, and that the just vengeance of the people might be awaiting him there. All the dark secrets of the torture-chamber, all the unpunished crimes of his class, warned him of coming vengeance, and filled his youthful, perhaps still immature, heart with such terror that he lost all power of clear thought and perception.

When the officers had had their say, they were led away so that the question might be debated in their absence.

I felt a sort of instinctive mistrust of them (possibly too, a prejudice of years against officers had something to do with it), and made a vigorous move against taking them into our ranks. I asked the question: Where had they been when the captain was preparing to shoot the sailors? Why had not the voice of conscience spoken in them then, and forced them to throw themselves on the captain and insist on his making an end of the persecution of the sailors?

But the speeches of several comrades, who argued that the cooperation of officers might be of great advantage to us, while the maintenance of a strict watch over them would "remove their poison-fangs," led the committee to grant their request, and they were released from arrest.

All the other officers were taken ashore next day.

****

Alexeieff had hardly given the order for the release of the officers, when some sailors ran in, crying that the whole port was in flames. The meeting broke up, and we all ran to the quarter-deck.

A terrible spectacle lay unfolded before our eyes. A vast glow of red lighted up almost the whole bay. Wherever one turned one's gaze, it met gigantic tongues of flame. They leapt ever higher and higher, and spread ever wider and wider, like beacons flashing the tidings of the all-devouring vengeance of the old *régime*.

This was not the red fire of the revolution; it was the white flame of the reaction! . . . Frenzied cries rose over this sea of fire. Suddenly there was a strange "*trra-tata*."

"They are firing on the people!" broke from all. And like madmen, filled with horror for our helpless unarmed brothers who were being destroyed, we ran to and fro, not knowing what to do, what to attempt. All were seized with one impulse—to cut short those orgies of horror, even at the price of our own lives. But how? Fire on the town? Fire where? Could we fire into that hell? What if at once we slaughter our own comrades? And the mind, sickened at the thought, beat about in hideous impotence.

There was frenzy and horror. Those men were dying in thousands for us, while we, strong and armed, stood aloof in safety with folded hands. . . .

At this awful moment, when the cowardliest were made brave, when the most vacillating were ready to face anything only to save the suffering, Alexeieff showed himself in all his worthlessness. While with bated breath we listened to volley after volley, and after each a cry of despair burst from us, he suddenly came up to us and said:

"What nonsense you are talking! That firing? It's simply the roofs cracking in the fire."

At that fearful moment the wretch, trembling for his own life, bethought himself that by giving aid to our brothers we might bring him into trouble; in those hours of madness he could still think of his safety and the decorations he would win; on that night of blood he could stake the life of thousands and cast them away to die rather than save them! . . . And to do this he did not hesitate at this murderous falsehood.

Fool! Pitiful coward! Your life may be saved, but your country, in its coming freedom, will cover it with the disgrace of banishment. It will brand your brow with the mark of Cain, and the awful hatred and contempt of men will make your life bitter and hard to bear.

Alexeieff's statement, made in a tone of authority, reassured us somewhat. But soon the experienced ear of the sailors made out the shots again, and again our hearts were filled with despair. As though afraid of that horror, we all spoke in whispers. We were afraid to breathe freely, to speak a word aloud.

So, we passed that awful night of massacre. Not one of us even thought of sleep.

One more little detail before concluding my account of the first day of the *Potemkins* presence at Odessa. When the port was already in flames, our sloop set off for the shore to try to learn whether we could not in some way help the workers. When they were near the breakwater, someone began hallooing to the sailors, and they came alongside.

It turned out to be a soldier of a marine battalion, who was coming to us to inform us in the name of the battalion of their complete solidarity with us.

So, a large part of the troops in Odessa had openly expressed their sympathy with the rising. And yet the legal gentleman who came from Moscow to my prison to conduct my preliminary examination assured me that "the army was loyal!"

Chapter 5
The Second Day

At five o'clock in the morning, physically and morally exhausted, I sat in a low chair in the admiral's stateroom and fell asleep.

I was soon awakened by a loud, indignant voice speaking near me. I jumped up, and found a group of sailors in the cabin and our medical officer in the midst of them. He was speaking warmly, insisting that the crew must send at once to the town for the funeral of Vakulintchuk. A sloop had come out with the news that a battle had been raging all night over the corpse between the police and the workmen, and that many of the workers had been killed in this unequal combat.

"We can't let people go on being killed for the sake of a dead man; we must bury him and make an end of it. If no one will go with me, I am going alone," he said excitedly.

I tried to calm him; and, feeling the justice of his words, I insisted on the committee's being summoned. The committee decided to send a deputation to the town to ask the governor for permission to bury Vakulintchuk.

I was among those who offered to join the deputation. I may be censured for taking part in such risky enterprise when my presence on the ship was indispensable; but we had to show the sailors that we were as ready in act as in word to lay down our lives for their cause. This, indeed, was what led me to offer to go.

In a moment they had furnished me with a singlet, a sailor's shirt and breeches; and, casting off my smart suit, I was transformed into a typical sailor. Saying goodbye to the crew, and warmly pressing the hand of Comrade A., I jumped into the sloop, where the other sailors were already sitting.

"Well, now we are off, brothers," I said to them.

"But we are waiting for the 'father.'"

"What do we want him for?"

"To perform the service for the dead; and, besides, we shall find it better going to the town with a priest: they will see at once that we have come with peaceable intentions."

The priest soon joined us. This minister of God presented a pitiful appearance. During the mutiny somebody had hit him on the nose with a chair, and the bandage would not keep in place on his thick, fleshy nose. It was coming down every minute, and he was entirely absorbed in dealing with it.

With a few more words of farewell to our comrades we sailed off.

An ominous stillness hung over the bay, usually so noisy and full of life. We came upon only one boat—the one that had brought the news of the fighting over the body. The workmen in it had not succeeded in landing the previous day, and now, in terror of being shot, had spent the whole night on the water.

We reached the land at the spot where the corpse was lying. The whole shore was lined with smoking ruins, with here and there a red tongue of flame leaping out. On all sides was death and desolation; only by the corpse there were a few workmen sitting. In spite of the menace of bullets and the danger of fire, they had been there all night guarding the corpse and the money collected for the funeral of Vakulintchuk.

We went on shore, and the priest proceeded to perform a service over the body. When Vakulintchuk's body was uncovered, it was horrible to look at him. The heat of the fire had hastened decomposition, and the body was black; a terrible stench came from it. The features so dear to the sailors were fearfully changed, and with dismay they made haste to cover them. . . .

There was no time to be lost in going to the governor; but it was impossible to enter the town from there, as the road was blocked with smoking ruins. So, we got into our boat again, and landed at a more convenient place.

The deputation consisted of two sailors and me. The name of one of them I don't know; the other, a sailor called K., was one of the men most devoted to the cause of revolution. He belonged to the small number of sailors on the *Potemkin* who had been members of the Social Democratic organisation before the outbreak of the mutiny. He could always be completely relied upon—was as firm as a rock. It was unfortunate that at the most critical moments he had been in the machinery department of the ship.

We set off without arms, and accompanied by the priest. I cannot refrain from recording here one comic episode, showing the terror inspired by the guns of the *Potemkin* in the gallant Cossacks. Scarcely had our little band entered the port when we came upon five Cossacks. We decided to approach them to inquire where we could find the commander of the troops. But as soon as the Cossacks noticed us, they turned and fled. In vain we shouted to them that we had no weapons, that the priest was with us. The gallant warriors would not listen, but flew from us on wings of terror.

Laughing at this exhibition, we began to ascend the steps to the Nikolaevsky Boulevard. There we were at once observed approaching, and a great excitement arose. We could see soldiers being drawn up, and officers running to and fro. We moved calmly and deliberately upwards. Only for a moment we stood still in horror as we almost stumbled over the body of a workman lying on the steps.

The youthful face was drawn with terror. On the chest there were stains of blood. Probably the treacherous bullet had struck him in the breast at the moment when he was running up the steps to escape from the bullets of the harbour soldiers. It was evident he had been the only one running by that way, as there were no traces of blood or other dead bodies. And here, alone, helpless, unarmed, flying in terror, he had been shot down like a wildfowl by the slaves of the *Tsar*. . . .

We three looked at one another while the gentle minister of the Lord stepped calmly on. We could do nothing, and had no alternative but to follow him. At last we arrived at the top.

We found a detachment of soldiers and a group of officers standing facing us. One of them stepped forward, came up to the priest, took him by the arm, and saying to him, "We will treat you with all reverence," drew him on one side. Then he gave the order to surround us. Instantly we were encircled by a forest of bayonets. I attempted to speak, and informed the officer that we had come to ask permission for the funeral of the dead sailor.

"All right; all right," was all he said in reply, and with the priest he retreated to the palace of the commander-in-chief of the troops (which is in the Nikolaevsky Boulevard).

It became evident to me that we should be shot that day.

I must confess that a feeling of horror came over me as I realised this. The military aspect of the boulevard, the guns' mouths pointing at us, the vindictive faces of the officers, all the surroundings, like the camp of a ferocious enemy, gave me a feeling of dismay.

This was increased by the sense of the stupidity of dying for a matter really of little consequence; we could quite well have buried the sailor at sea with all ceremony and reverence.

But I felt that I was facing an enemy, to whom one cannot show oneself alarmed, or he will devour one. I quickly pulled myself together, and my face was so calm that K. told me afterwards that he wondered at my composure.

We had not long to wait. Soon the same officer reappeared and addressed us in quite a different tone.

Sailors, your holy father has gone to the governor to ask permission; you go into the courtyard of the commander's palace. We do not put you under arrest; no, this is simply to avoid exciting the attention of the public.

Still, we were escorted by soldiers into the courtyard, which was filled with Cossacks. K., who was himself of Cossack origin, began inquiring of the Cossacks whether there was no one among them who came from his village. But the Cossacks passed by in silence, and did not vouchsafe a reply to the mutineer.

Such treatment of a fellow-countryman, whom they would perhaps shoot down in another moment, wounded K.'s honest and upright heart. He said:

Ekh, you are Cains, not men. Here, I'm going to be hanged, maybe, in a moment, and I want to send greetings home, and you run from me as though I were a leper. But for whose sake are we going to our death? Is it for our own? . .

And the words flowed hotly from his lips. They were full of bitterness and anger at the soldiers ready to fire on their own comrades. At the end he could not control his feelings, and burst into tears.

They were not tears of cowardice that he shed; they were the tears of an honest heart, wounded by the wickedness and hatred of his fellows.

His fiery words went home even to the Cossacks. They began to gather round him, ceased jesting, and listened to him with serious faces; some even began to justify themselves. "It's not we; it's the government does it all; do we do it of ourselves? It's the officer's orders."

I wanted to answer them when the rattle of a shot made us start. They all smiled.

"That's nothing, don't be frightened, brothers. That's only firing in the air, scaring the people."

Every fifteen minutes we heard such firing. We began talking with the soldiers and Cossacks again about the position of affairs in Odessa, and learnt some important news. Troops were being concentrated on Odessa from all parts. A whole regiment with mortars would arrive today from Kishineff. Tomorrow troops were coming from Nikolaieff. Garrison artillery was expected. Every hour the enemy was regaining lost ground and increasing its strength. The later we were in taking action, the greater the opposing force we should have to meet. I resolved, if I were so lucky as to get back to the ironclad, to begin at once a zealous advocacy of active measures. But should I get back? There was still no sign of the priest, and we were beginning to suspect some trap.

But at last the priest actually made his appearance, and we heaved a sigh of relief. Everything became clear and reassuring at once. The priest came up to us with a colonel.

"Permission is given you to bury the sailor at two o'clock in the night," the latter informed us; "the daytime is out of the question."

I knew this would make the sailors indignant, and I answered aloud with dignity:

"Our comrade is not a thief—to be buried at night."

"Well, that's your affair," answered the colonel, "and now you can go."

The autocracy was true to itself; aware of the awe-inspiring force behind as, it dared not arrest us, and so displayed an astounding magnanimity.

I need hardly say that we lost no time in acting on the colonel's suggestion, and making our way back to the port.

As we were coming away from the steps, we met a funeral procession. This was very fortunate, as we had to order a coffin for Vakulintchuk. After arranging this with the undertaker, we made our way to our sloop, going this time by another road, full of horror; there were corpses lying in numbers on it, and we had to walk carefully not to step on them. All of them were scorched by fire.

Workmen who met us on the road described the shooting of the previous day.

Meetings had been held in the port all the preceding day. A platform was put up near the body of Vakulintchuk. One speaker after another called the people in stirring speeches to a resolute struggle with *Tsarism*. Thousands of people were coming and going in the port. A sort of delirious enthusiasm prevailed; people embraced each other, and stripped themselves of all they had for the common cause. Masses of wealth, stores of provisions and wines, lay piled up on the ground, but no one dared to desecrate those sacred hours by robbing. Order and tranquillity were general everywhere. In one place a hooligan shouted: "Beat the Jews!" He was instantly killed.

At four o'clock the representatives of the Social Democratic societies, who had been on the *Potemkin*, reached the shore. One of them ascended the platform, explained that the sailors were not going to land, and begged the people to disperse quietly to their homes, and to attempt nothing till the *Potemkin* took action.

The workers began slowly moving out of the port, singing the "*Varshavianka*." But the rush of crowds to the port did not cease.

The retreating workmen were met by thousands of the inhabitants of the town. Smartly dressed *bourgeois*, clean and dapper shopkeepers, filled the places vacated by the workmen. They, too, wanted to be present at the first meetings of the people; they were carried along by the general enthusiasm into forgetting their fears.

But with the departure of the workmen, the organising force which maintained order left the port. The police, too, were actively at work, promoting pillage. Soon there was heard the sound of breaking in casks of spirit.

The organised workmen who were still in the crowd did their utmost to combat disorder. They rolled the casks of spirit into the sea. But the elements of disorder were aroused; nothing could hold them back.

In one place there was the glow of fire, in another part men were picking over heaps of expensive goods and stuffing them in their pockets. The flames spread all the while; millions of *roubles*' worth of goods were burnt; men, too, who had got drunk on the costly wines, were burnt to death.

Meanwhile the port was resounding with the rattle of bullets from the troops and the wailing of the wounded. The crowd made a rush for the town, but there they were met by fresh volleys of shots. The Cossacks let no one escape, cutting them down with their sabres and driving them back. And forced back by them, the crowd was driven closer and closer to the water's edge; many were thrust into the sea and drowned.

Horror and madness reigned there; the sea and the air were filled with blood, and the "red laugh" of blood hung over the earth.

Full of dismay at this awful picture, we made our way in silence to the sloop and sailed to the ship, leaving a guard of five men by the corpse.

My reply to the colonel was not an empty phrase; the sailors really were unwilling to bury their comrade by night. To send another deputation to ask for permission to bury him by day they thought risky, and many declared that Vakulintchuk's body might be cast into the sea with all the funeral ceremonies, and that comrades could not be sacrificed on account of a funeral. I was inclined to take that view myself; but, as the reader will see later, the frightened generals did not wait for our decision.

It was nearly dinner-time.

Matushenko set off to take provisions to the sailors who were watching the corpse on the shore.

Kirill, A., and I were together, discussing the position in the light of the news I had brought. We had just decided to urge the crew to take resolute action against the town, when we were interrupted by a loud shout: "The squadron!" and a tremendous hubbub. We hardly had time to find out what was happening, when the whistle summoned the committee, and we rushed to the admiral's stateroom. We learned that a wreath of smoke and the flag of a man-of-war had been seen in the distance.

The deliberations of the committee did not last long. Kirill and I spoke.

"Don't let us lose our heads; let us stand firmly at our posts and meet the enemy boldly and with dignity. The people are with us, truth is with us, strength is with us. Let us go boldly to battle for 'freedom,'" one of us concluded his speech.

"For freedom!" the committee shouted, like one man, and everyone rushed to his place.

The admiral's stateroom was left empty. We went out on to the quarter-deck.

A curl of smoke could be seen in the distance. The alarm was just going to be sounded, but the signalman shouted that it was the *Pruth*, and that it was turning its course towards Nikolaieff. (The signalman performs duties of great responsibility. He pilots the ship during the voyage, gives the gunners their aim in firing, carries on communication by semaphore, etc.) The more developed and intelligent of the sailors are appointed, as a rule, for this duty. Someone suggested pursuing and capturing it, to which the reply was made that it was a swift ship, and could not be overtaken. And so, the *Pruth*, though it passed so near us, did not join us, since it did not know of our revolt. This incident, of no great significance in itself, showed us the excitement with which the sailors were expecting the squadron. At the least puff of smoke from a man-of-war, they fancied the whole squadron at hand.

The excitement had completely subsided when Matushenko arrived with good tidings. The authorities had sanctioned the funeral at two o'clock in the day. The funeral procession might be escorted by a guard of honour of twelve sailors, whose safety would be guaranteed. And thus, the question of the funeral was settled very simply and creditably for us.

The soldiers who brought this authorisation had come to the sailors not only with a message from their officers, but also to tell them from the soldiers of their sympathy with the sailors. But they told the latter that their counsels were divided, and they were afraid to begin. Let the sailors take the first step, and the garrison of Odessa would go over to the side of the people.

A military council was being held, they said, in the theatre of the town. Let the sailors shell the theatre, and they would kill all the generals. Then the soldiers would lay down their rifles and join us.

Matushenko completely agreed with this plan, and resolved to carry it out. This unexpected support from a man of such influence with the crew made our task much easier. We decided to summon a committee at once.

At first our efforts in committee met with complete success. We managed to rouse them to the point of deciding to begin the bombardment that day. The following plan of action was formed: We were to fire three blank charges to warn the inhabitants, and two shells at the theatre, after which a deputation of three men should go to the town and lay the following demands before the commander-in-chief:

1. The immediate release of all political prisoners;

2. The immediate cessation of firing on the peaceable inhabitants of the town; and

3. As guarantee of this the withdrawal of all troops from the town and the surrender of the arsenals to the people.

If the authorities should refuse to grant our demands, we would begin bombarding the town next day. If the soldiers should join us today, we would at once take possession of the town, and make it the base from which to carry on the revolution.

Though the committee accepted the whole plan without reservation, they were yet unwilling to take so grave a step without the approval of the whole crew, and it was decided to call a general assembly. The roll-call was sounded, and the sailors began to assemble on the quarter-deck.

These mass assemblies made an interesting picture. The front rows sat round as in an amphitheatre, the next rows stood, and behind them others stood on raised supports. Sailors sat in careless attitudes on the huge towers and monstrous mouths of the 12-inch guns. The scene was bright with the clean white shirts of the sailors. Their manly figures were breathing with health and vigour. All their faces were serious and thoughtful. In the centre of the ring stood two capstans, and from them the speakers and the chairman spoke.

Properly speaking, such assemblies had no regularly chosen chairman, but Dymtchenko or some one of the more influential sailors usually performed the functions of one.

On this occasion it was Dymtchenko, who rose and uttered his habitual simple-hearted phrase: "Here, lads, a good man wants to say a word to you."

I got on to the capstan and began to speak. First of all, I reminded the sailors that they had already crossed the line beyond which there was no hoping for pardon. They had burnt their boats; the Rubicon was crossed. There could be no reconciliation with *Tsarism* now. Only the victory of one side and the complete annihilation of the other could settle the matter, so it must be war to the bitter end. We must unite with the strongest allies; we must deal the enemy a deadly blow. The troops in Odessa were ready to come over to us; they were only waiting for the first step. This step the sailors must take.

While the enemy was still in confusion, before he had gathered his forces together, we must deal a decisive blow. Every minute he was growing stronger and drawing in fresh reinforcements. The first panic was passing over, and with it the chance of overwhelming the enemy by one determined blow would pass away. Every moment of delay was strengthening the enemy and weakening us. Hence the conclusion: we must proceed to resolute action at once. And then I acquainted the sailors with the plan we had elaborated.

And during all this speech I asked the sailors after every statement whether they agreed with it. "True," rang out every time. When I finished speaking, my voice was drowned in a deafening "Hurrah!" It seemed as though the thing was done, and we had only to pass a definite resolution in accordance with the general feeling. But suddenly I heard the phrase: "Fire on the town we can't!"

Someone took it up; then several voices chimed in, and soon a considerable proportion of the crew were shouting that we couldn't fire on the town.

Kirill came up to me and said: "You went to work too abruptly; it can't be done like that."

I saw myself now that I had been injudicious in telling them straight out of the plan. That ought to have been left to one of the sailors. The feeling of the mistake I had made reduced me to despair. When such a matter was in the balance, to risk failure was almost a crime.

While I was fuming inwardly, the crew were in violent excitement, divided into two parties, one insisting on the immediate bombardment of the town, the other protesting against it. And the latter was beginning to get the upper hand. Cries were even heard of "Away with the landsmen!" "Let the officers have their say!"

All eyes were turned on Alexeieff, but he was silent. He was silent in spite of the fact that his word might have given the victory to his party. He was silent because his feeble spirit was afraid to face the conflict of passions.

At that moment Matushenko sprang on the capstan. His appearance silenced the shouts of wrangling at once.

He began:

> Stay, brothers, here I see quarrels have arisen among us. Things have come to such a pass with us that one half of the crew is turning against the other. We must have unity, and here it is coming to sailors taking up their rifles and killing one another. No, lads, you can't do so! Our rulers have done enough setting us against each other, and now you want to fall to killing of yourselves. The whole people is looking to you now; it is looking for you as its deliverers, and here you are quarrelling among yourselves.

And his words flowed on, full of simple eloquence and pity for the oppressed, long-suffering people. It was the tribune of the people speaking now, pouring out in simple words the people's suffering, the pent-up woe of a thousand years.

And at these words the hearts of all were brimming over with anger and hatred for the oppressors of long ages. Soon it was no longer the tribune of the people, but the sailor, who spoke with full understanding of the psychology of his comrades.

> Here there are three hundred of us Social Democrats on the ship. We have resolved to lay down our lives for the cause of the people, and to fight for it to the last drop of our blood. If you don't want to fire, we will go to the guns ourselves and send

our threatening bombs at the *Tsar*. And you, if you want to, join us, or else take your rifles and shoot us all down; or else bind us and hand us over to the authorities. They will welcome you with music, reward you with decorations. . . ."

"No, we won't have that!" the crew roared, suddenly roused by this picture.

"Now, then, do you agree to fire on the town?"

"We agree!" shouted the sailors; and now not one voice dared interpose a protest in this outburst of united feeling in the mass.

"Maybe someone does not agree, but his voice is not heard," Matushenko went on relentlessly, "so let us do this: those who are for firing go to the right, and those against, to the left."

The whole crew moved to the right.

"There, you see what mean souls there are among you? They'll stir the crew up behind one's back, so as not to be seen, but are afraid to give their opinion openly."

The "conductors" were abashed.

"Well, brothers, now stand steady. Go to your places."

The crew dispersed about the ship with renewed energy, and began to make ready for action. The machinists ran to the machinery department, the marine gunners ran to clean the guns, the rest of the sailors fell to clearing the decks. The medical staff got the ambulance and first-aid appliances in readiness. The doctor made the *Viekha* ready as an ambulance.

Before the meeting we had sent twelve sailors to the town for the funeral. Now voices were raised protesting against firing before our men had returned, for fear of killing them. This most reasonable consideration was, however, overlooked in the general confusion.

It was five o'clock in the evening when the battle alarm sounded. I had never been on a man-of-war during manoeuvres, and was now impressed by the discipline and rapidity with which everything was done.

The bugle sounded. The sailors standing near me ran off, and the exposed parts of the ship were suddenly left empty; while men were running with extraordinary swiftness about the ladders and the spar-deck. Within three minutes all was quiet, the big guns were loaded, and the gunners were standing at each gun. The approaches to the admiral's stateroom were closed by iron hatchways, and it was some time before I could realise where I was. A moment before the stairs to the admiral's room had been here, and now they were gone.... All of a sudden, my feet were drenched with cold water; the hoses were left running that the wooden floor of the deck might not catch fire from the shells. I beat a hasty retreat into the inner part of the ship. Here, too, I was struck by the marvellous order. Everyone stood at his post, and there was not one sailor to be seen unoccupied.

Pointing out the theatre to the signalman, I made my way to the bridge, from which they were keeping a watch on the town with a telescope. There I found Kovalenko and a sailor I will call Z., who told me they were going to fire from the 6-inch guns.

Then we heard the signal sounded, and the boom of the first blank shot. Then a second and a third. The first shell was to follow a quarter of an hour later.

A feeling of terror and of joy clutched at my heart in these moments. We had advanced at last to action. Who could tell what was before us? And if our shells were to fall not on the theatre, but on the houses of peaceable citizens and, instead of happiness, we were bringing desolation and destruction on the people? ... And awful pictures rose before my mind. ... But soon they passed, and I saw instead the picture of the people's revolution. Behind the smoke of the shot, just floating out, I seemed to see the red battalions of the army of the revolution, marching victoriously, ever farther and farther into the heart of Russia. Behind the crash of the first shell I seemed to hear the triumph and rejoicing of the conquering people.

The bugle sounded. All was quiet. Then a flash of bright light followed by a deafening roar—the echo went on sounding long after it. Again, a hush, interrupted by the harsh shout, "Overshot!" from the signalman standing beside me. Before our minds rose the picture of women and children buried under the fragments of the bursting shell.

But now again we heard the signal; and after it the deafening roar, and again the same ear-splitting shout of the signalman, "Overshot!"

Our shells had missed their mark; the hands of the *Tsar's* servant, the base traitor, had turned them from the enemies of the people. They did not shatter the walls of the theatre; but they shattered another stouter and stronger wall—the wall of the soldiers' barracks. And through the breach the fire of revolution broke in and consumed the whole edifice of military discipline, and the last relics of loyal feeling. And their deafening report echoed over all Russia from the Black to the Baltic Sea, from the Caucasus to Siberia, and everywhere it awakened the slumbering Russian soldier from the unbroken sleep of ages.

★★★★★★★★★

We were deeply distressed at the failure of our brief bombardment. It seemed likely that our shells had dropped on the houses of peaceful citizens, and caused the misery of those for whom we were fighting. We all rushed up to the signalman Vedermeier, asking why the shells had missed their aim. He, without the least hesitation, replied that to get a correct aim you must have a map to scale. There were none among us specialists able to criticize this; and, besides, no one suspected the possibility of treachery, or thought of controverting his statement.

It was only later, in Theodosia, that one of the officers in charge of me. Lieutenant Pomerantsev, told me that the incorrect aim had been given by Vedermeier intentionally. I should not have given much credit to his words except for the simple reflection that in battles at sea there is no map of the position of the enemy's ships, and yet the shells do hit them. When I met abroad some comrades who had been with me in the rising, they confirmed the statement made by Pomerantsev. Then I learned, too, of another treacherous action on the part of Vedermeier. On the evening of the day when we bombarded the town, some soldiers on the coast signalled to us:

Keep up the bombardment; in the morning we will join you.

Vedermeier received this signal, but concealed it from the crew. . . .

Vedermeier returned from Roumania to Russia, where, of course, not a sentence and a halter, but a reward awaited him. But he will not escape the judgment of free Russia, and her avenging hand will punish the traitor according to his deserts. . . .

We believed Vedermeier, and resolved to procure such a map; meanwhile we ran to the wardroom, to which the committee was being summoned by the whistle, for the election of the deputation to the commander-in-chief. I was chosen, and with me two sailors whose names it is not convenient to give. The cutter was got ready, and, taking a solemn farewell of our comrades, who promised to open fire from all the guns, if we should not come back, we set off.

Twilight had set in; the last faint rays of the dying day were sinking into the slumbering sea. Everything spoke of the passing day, everything was full of a quiet yearning melancholy. And in spite of myself mournful thoughts of my own life, so soon to pass away, came upon me. . . .

A private sloop with two sailors came rowing towards us. The sailors in it were Mikishkin and a comrade returning from the funeral of Vakulintchuk. Mikishkin was a tall, spare man, always serious, with great dreamy eyes, always fixed on some point in the far distance. In his dirty, greasy jacket, that contrasted so strangely with the snow-white shirts of the other sailors, he looked more like a philosopher than a marine. He was always to be seen with Father Petroff's pamphlet in his hand, discoursing to the sailors on the religious and political views of that priest. His speech was quick and hurried, but his audience was not always an attentive one, and sometimes, when he came down from the clouds, he would find not one left listening to him.

This did not, however, greatly trouble him, and he would soon be talking away somewhere else. But he was not altogether deluded by the philosophy of love; he knew very well that there are enemies, who must be influenced, not by words, but by force. Throughout the whole rising, both in the committee and among the crew, he championed the boldest measures, and always volunteered to assist in carrying them out. On this occasion he had offered to be one of the funeral procession.

"Why are you two here? Where are the others?" Matushenko, who was in command of the cutter, asked him.

"O, brothers, they've been firing at us," Mikishkin began to tell us in his rapid way. "On the way there it was all right, they didn't touch us; but on the way back, as we were coming down from the bridge, a company of soldiers stood there. We took no notice, we went on; all at once they banged away at us! ... We up and ran. The lucky thing is the little soldiers didn't aim straight at us; bullets went popping between our legs, and not one of them hit us."

"Where are the others?"

"Six are waiting on the shore, and four ran away to the town."

"When did they fire on you? Was it before or after our shells?" I asked, supposing that our bombardment was the reason of this treacherous shooting. But, to my surprise, Mikishkin replied that the sailors heard the explosion of our shells while they were running to the shore.

"And where are you going, brothers," Mikishkin asked us.

We told him.

"Oh, don't go, brothers!" he said earnestly, seeming quite scared for a moment. "They'll shoot you, for a certainty."

We went on, of course, without heeding Mishkin's warnings.

But his apprehensions were not groundless; if the authorities had failed to keep their word, and had fired on sailors to whom they had promised security, they would be in such a fury after our bombardment that they would be hardly likely to spare us, who were coming with revolutionary demands.

But we had not long to deliberate. The cutter had by now reached the shore, and we landed. Here we found six more sailors and a few workmen, who had been hanging about for the last two days among the smouldering ruins. When we told them that we were going to the commander of the troops, they informed us that a cordon of soldiers had been placed round the port, and instructions had been given to fire at any sailor who dared make his appearance, as the authorities were afraid after the bombardment that the *Potemkin* would land men and make a descent on the town.

Though we were unarmed and carried a white flag, still the soldiers might not observe this, and might fire on us before we had time to explain the object of our coming. I therefore suggested going first to a church in the port, and getting the priest to go to the commander of the troops to give him notice of our coming. The others all agreed to this plan, and we made our way to the church.

After the din of our shells, we were especially struck by the death-like stillness in the port: not a sound, as though everything were dead. We heard nothing but here and there the crash of burning houses as they fell in. Corpses blackened by fire still lay untouched along the road; and we were haunted by the foreboding that soon, perhaps, in the town we might find that same fearful sight, caused not by the autocracy, but by ourselves. As though to confirm our fears, at the moment when we reached the church the "first aid" ambulance drove by at a gallop. We went into the church enclosure, and found there a woman and some children. They were the priest's wife and family.

We asked her to fetch the holy father; but the poor woman, alarmed by the events that had taken place almost before her eyes during the last few days, was terrified at the sight of us, and with a shaky voice began begging us not to hurt the priest.

"He loves the poor; he is always doing good to the working man," she urged.

We made haste to reassure her, and explained the object of our visit. But we had much ado to persuade her to fetch the priest.

The priest, a tall man, with a mild and kindly face, which wore a look of fatigue and suffering, consented at once to do what we asked. He mounted the steps to the *boulevard*, while we stayed behind in the church and began to ask his wife for news. But as she had not gone out during the last few days at all, she knew nothing of what was happening in the town, and where our shells had fallen. She told us a great deal, however, about the horrors of the previous night in the port.

Meanwhile the priest returned and told us that the authorities consented to receive us, and guaranteed that we should not be touched. Thanking him, we went our way up the steps.

On the very topmost landing we saw, sitting in an armchair, a short general, with a grey beard and sharp features, surrounded by a complete retinue of officers. (To the best of my recollection, we were told that this was the second in command of the troops—General Protopopov; but in my "act of accusation" it was stated that it was the temporary Governor-General of Odessa—Karangozov.)

The comrade who carried the flag lowered it, according to custom, at the feet of the general, after which the latter asked us what we had come for.

I answered him:

"We have fired two shells today as a demonstration that we may take decisive action at any moment; but we do not desire unnecessary bloodshed. And therefore, we invite the commander of the troops to come out to us on the ship, or to send some fully authorised person to hear our demands."

"And if we do not accede to this request?"

"Then we consider ourselves free to take action."

"Very well; I will report your request to the commander-in-chief."

"One point further," I put in, as he was getting up; "if we do not return to the ship by ten o'clock, they will open fire from all the guns."

The general and the officers seemed startled. . . .

"I will report everything to the commander-in-chief," said the general, and he withdrew.

We stood waiting.

The colonel of Cossacks who had talked to us in the morning came up, and began looking at us attentively. Seeing me, he said: "Oh, this one was here this morning!"

Another colonel came up too, and asked us what we had done with the officers who still survived. Before we had time to answer the inquisitive colonel, a general came up and, shouting angrily at the officer, forbade him to speak to us.

"I merely asked one question, Your Excellency," the colonel explained, with a guilty air.

"Not one word must be said to them," bawled the general, and the colonel moved away.

I can't tell why the gallant general said this. Was it because we were here for a parley, and he remembered the rules of such negotiations, or did he think it degrading to the uniform for an officer to speak with traitors to the *Tsar?* ...

About fifteen minutes later the first general returned, and gave us the following reply from the commander-in-chief:

"The commander-in-chief does not desire to enter into any negotiations with mutineers; and if you like to fire more shells at the houses of peaceful citizens, then God and the *Tsar* will be your judges. Now you can go—no one will touch you."

The haughty tone of this answer enraged us, but we resolved to express our indignation in acts, not in words. We turned and went away.

In the port we shouted to the sailors in the cutter and, getting into it, we returned to the ship.

The sailors were eagerly awaiting our return, and crowded after us into the wardroom, where the committee was sitting. There was complete silence all around us as we repeated the commander-in-chief's reply. As might well be expected, it aroused a storm of indignation.

"We'll show him whether we are mutineers! He won't talk to us, then let him talk to the 12-inch guns." Angry threats came in a continuous stream from the sailors. But the chairman imposed silence on all, and called on one of the sailors who had taken part in the funeral to speak.

His description of the enthusiastic reception given them by the people, and the treacherous shots fired at the sailors, added fuel to the fire. The passions of the mass were kindled. The excitement was growing, and it was clear that by dawn next day they would be ready to begin decisive action against the town. But even in this resolute mood there was an "if only" very characteristic of the temper of the men.

"*If only* the squadron would come, he wouldn't talk to us like that," said the sailors.

Chapter 6

The Third Day

This "if only" expressed the intense eagerness with which the squadron was expected. When they mutinied, the sailors looked for the revolt of the whole squadron, of which there were vague rumours in the air. They were convinced not only that the squadron would refuse to fire on them, but that it would come over to them. With the whole squadron at their back they had nothing to fear: that would be a force too mighty for the autocracy to deal with. With the squadron would be victory, without it defeat.

Such reliance on the squadron as the factor that would decide the fate of the rising was perilous in the extreme for the revolution. What if their hopes should not be justified?—if the squadron did not join them?—if the crews were being so weeded out that the sailors left would fire on them? Then the totally unexpected failure of their hopes would be the ruin of their cause; for if the garrison in defence of a fortress be not strong in its spirit of self-confidence, the feeblest enemy can take it without difficulty.

It was our task to instil into the sailors the idea that they were an independent and mighty force of themselves, and that they must look for help not to the squadron, but to the people. Slowly, step by step, we were influencing the minds of the mass. The sailors were beginning already to feel their strength, and were making up their minds to act independently. And it was only owing to our efforts and the events of those first two days that the *Potemkin* met the squadron so proudly and steadily, fully determined to conquer or to perish....

The thoughts of all the crew were centred on the squadron: on all hands we could hear discussion as to the whereabouts of the squadron. This question fretted and excited everyone. We stopped every vessel we saw on the sea; every man-of-war we caught sight of we hailed as the squadron. The word was always on our lips. (See above the account of the sighting of the *Viekha* and of the *Pruth*.)

And the committee was incessantly discussing the question. What was to be done on meeting the squadron? The plan approved by them rested on the fighting superiority of the *Potemkin*, whose guns were better fitted for distant firing than those of the other ironclads. It was proposed that, when the squadron came within range of our guns, the order should be given it to stand still on pain of our opening fire. If the order were obeyed, we would send a torpedo-boat to negotiate with the crews. If the squadron were to continue advancing towards us, we would open fire on it, while ourselves still out of range of its guns. In this way, before the squadron would be in a position to act against us, it would be so weakened that we should be able to cope with it.

This plan, perfectly suitable on meeting the ships of an enemy prepared for battle, might be fatal to our cause. It overlooked the circumstance that the sailors were not dreaming of fighting with us, that the only enemy we had to face was to be found in the officers. It was essential that the first order to fire should come from them—then the sailors would revolt, and the squadron would be in our hands; whereas if the first shot came from us, fired not only at the officers, but at the sailors who were in sympathy with us, the instinct of self-preservation would drive the latter to take up arms against us.

But not a single objection of this kind was raised in the committee. My plan was accepted, and instructions were given to Alexeieff in accordance with it. The plan was not, however, carried into effect, and this we were spared, thanks to—Alexeieff. It was, of course, not from sympathy with our aims that he let the squadron get so close to us without giving the order to fire; his action was due, I imagine, to very different motives.

The morning of the next day opened for me with the magical words, "The squadron!" which, shouted in the wardroom, waked me up. In the wardroom there were standing about fifteen men, and the telegraphist was telling them of a telegram he had caught by the wireless telegraph. It consisted of the two words, "distinctly visible," and came from the *Rostislav*. This was enough to show that the squadron was near.

The committee had already been summoned, and was soon assembled. The former plan was recapitulated in its general features, and instructions were given to the crew to get the ship ready for action.

Everyone set eagerly to work. The sailors, hearing that the long-expected squadron was at hand, worked with a will. Those who had nothing to do clustered round the telegraph installation, hoping another telegram might be received....

This hope was realised, for very soon another telegram was captured. It was from the *Rostislav* to the *Three Bishops*, and ran as follows:

"We are telegraphing to you at the distance of five...."

At that point the telegram broke off. This was very unfortunate, as if we had known what distance the ironclads were from one another, it might have given us a clue to what they were doing. The mere number five, with no indication of the unit of measurement, told us nothing. It was clear, in any case, that the squadron was not far off....

Then somebody was struck with a happy thought—to seize one of the fast steamers at anchor in the roads, and, hiding some sailors on board of it, to send it off to reconnoitre. Two hours later (at nine o'clock in the morning) the steamer returned with the news that the squadron was approaching.

In a short time, the signalman could make out the smoke through the telescope.

The alarm was sounded. Everyone was full of excitement and suspense. A great historical moment was at hand: what would it bring forth?

I stood with comrade A. on the captain's bridge, and, straining my eyes, tried to make out the squadron in the distance. Soon we could detect the smoke with the naked eye, and a little later the ironclads themselves were visible. There were three of them—the *Twelve Apostles*, the *Sinope*, and the *George the Victorious*, accompanied by a flotilla of torpedo-boats. Everything was in readiness in our ship; the gunners were at the guns, the charges were rolled there on wire. In the ambulances camp-beds were in readiness, and the medical staff stood with stretchers on the bridges.

Again, the alarm was sounded. The red flag of battle was unfurled, and the *Potemkin* in all her menacing readiness steamed gracefully out to meet the squadron.

There seemed a sort of muddle in the squadron. We could see the ships stop in their course and begin changing their positions in relation to one another. "They are being drawn up in fighting array," said a sailor standing near me.

But he took too flattering a view of the daring of the superior officers. It appeared that the ironclads were drawn up for retreat, not for fighting, as soon as the officers saw the *Potemkin* ready for battle. They turned and began moving away from us at full steam.

★★★★★★★★★★

Koshuba, a sailor of the *George the Victorious*, who afterwards came on our ship, gave a vivid description of the panic that seized the officers of the squadron when they saw the *Potemkin* coming towards them with the battle-flag flying. The officers ran about the ships in terror, crying that if the *Potemkin* began to fire, she would send them all to the bottom. The commander of the squadron gave the order to turn and steam for the open sea. The officers were continually running to the machinery department, begging the engineers to get up the top speed, and promising them money out of their own pockets. This description, given by such a man as Koshuba, may be believed without reservation, and, indeed, there is nothing in it inconsistent with what we know of the character of Russian officers.

★★★★★★★★★★

The idea occurred to me of attacking this part of the squadron before it had time to join the remaining battleships. We might promptly get up full steam, and pursue the squadron at our topmost speed, and then send them instructions to stand still, opening fire, and taking the ships by force, if they did not obey.

I ran to Alexeieff and proposed he should carry out this plan. But, needless to say, he declined to do so, alleging that these ironclads might be intentionally drawing us into the open sea, where the remainder of the squadron was in waiting.

This objection had no weight whatever, as we must in any case meet the squadron, if not immediately, a few hours later; and there was no advantage in our meeting the ships on the shore of Odessa rather than in the open sea. The retreating iron-clads were precisely those whose crews later on greeted us with shouts of "Hurrah!" Moreover, they were the oldest and weakest ironclads in the fleet. Being isolated from the other battleships, which were very powerful and hostilely disposed to the revolt, and being confronted by the overwhelming might of the *Potemkin*, which could blow them into atoms if they refused to join her, and could give them efficient protection if they did join her, the crews of these ironclads would have thrown in their lot with us after the first shots fired by us, especially if our shots passed over them (I had laid stress on this point when I proposed my plan). If the control of the *Potemkin* had been in our hands at that moment, the squadron would have been ours, and the success of the rising might have been secured....

But Alexeieff was in command . . . and instead of pursuing the squadron, we returned to the harbour and cast anchor at the same place as before.

Then Dr. Golenko, who had been on the *Viekha*, came up to the *Potemkin* in a sloop, and, coming on board, rubbed his hands gleefully.

"Ah, how glad I am, friends, you have come back. I was afraid you had gone off without me. I am on your side, you know."

This time he was probably sincere in his joy at our return. He had not yet had time to do his job; and how could he have faced the authorities? They would not have been ready to take his word for it that he had stayed on to betray us. They are stern judges who look for acts and put no faith in words.

The doctor talked glibly of his delight, and tripped off to the groups of sailors to congratulate them on their first victory.

Though the squadron had fled from us, we were well aware that it might come back any minute with its full quota of vessels. We therefore lost no time in reviewing the fighting capacity of the ship. The committee sitting in the wardroom sent for the superintendents of the various parts of the ship, and inquired of them whether everything in their several departments was in readiness, or whether there was anything wanting. It appeared that the signalling men were running short of coal for the searchlights, and the engineers had not a sufficient supply of sulphuric acid.

These defects had to be made good at once, or the ship could not be put into perfect readiness for battle. We decided to send a sailor and comrade A. to the town to procure these articles. Dressed like ordinary residents, they set off in a private sloop and cautiously landed. Unhappily these comrades were not able to come back to us.

At this same committee meeting the plan of action was discussed once more. The simple-hearted sailor, M., proposed that on sighting the squadron again we should command the ironclads to stand still, and ask the admiral to come to us for a parley. When we had the admiral on board, we would send instructions in his name for all the officers to come to the *Potemkin* for a consultation with him. Then we would arrest them, and should have no difficulty in gaining control of the ships. If the admiral were to refuse to come to us, we would open fire. This proposition was adopted by the committee.

We had not long to wait for the second appearance of the squadron. At twelve o'clock five vessels came into sight.

Again, the battle-alarm was sounded and the red flag run up.

At the same moment we received by wireless telegraph the following message from Admiral Vishnevetsky:

"Black Sea men, appalled at your conduct. Surrender."

We replied:

"Squadron, stand at anchor; admiral to come on board for parley. Promise security."

The squadron advanced at the same pace upon us.

Again, a telegram flew to us:

"Madmen, what have you done? Surrender! The sword spares the penitent head."

In reply we dispatched again the previous telegram with the threatening addition:

"Else we shall fire."

On the *Rostislav* and the *Sinope* signals were raised for reversing the engines, but still the squadron continued to advance upon us.

The previous retreat of the squadron had immensely raised the sailors' spirits. It had shown them their own strength, and now they were possessed by feelings very different from the mood in which they had first seen the squadron approach. If the temper of the mass might have been described then by the word "tremulous," now it was calm in the serene confidence of strength. All were conscious of their own power and of the greatness of the moment, and every man was resolved to conquer or to die. They were not men worked up by nervous excitement or hypnotised by eloquence, ready at the first moment to dash into the fray, and afterwards as quickly to take to flight. No! These were veterans, self-possessed, and ready for anything. . . . The movements of the men were rapid, vigorous, but wonderfully deft; their faces impassive, dignified, while their eyes kept a bold and alert watch on the enemy. They were seven hundred picked men—seven hundred ready for death.

The immense squadron, with its death-dealing torpedo-boats, was bearing down upon us in a huge flock. In front were the strongest ironclads, the *Rostislav* and the *Three Bishops*.

All at once the *Potemkin* weighed anchor, and, serene and bold, as the spirit of her crew, she steamed proudly into the space between them. . . .

Everything on the two ships was in fighting trim; Nowhere was a sailor to be seen, but on the bridge of the *Rostislav* stood a group of officers.

Our guns slowly turned upon the retreating ships. Suddenly an immense 6-inch gun on the *Potemkin* was aimed at the bridge of the *Rostislav*, and the group of officers scattered away from it and vanished below.

There was a hush, a sudden hush, on our ship. The noise and shouts had died away, and the sailors in grim silence carried out the commands as they rang out.

I was again standing on the bridge, this time with Kirill. The first shot from the ironclads would have blown us to pieces, as we were standing on an open place. But during those days we had grown so used to the awful thought of death that nothing had terrors for us now. We stood there calmly, and were surprised ourselves at our own calmness. I almost felt ashamed that I should be so calm at such a moment, as though I were not fully conscious of its grandeur. I spoke of the feeling to Kirill, and he answered that he was feeling just the same.

And now the other ships were coming near. Again, the menacing guns glared at us on both sides. We were, as it were, in a fearful ring. . . .

But our guns, too, were glaring as fiercely at our foes, and keeping as close a watch on every one of them. A moment . . . and the sea might be echoing with the thunder of guns and shrieks of men, and stained red with blood. But instead of the fearful roar of cannon, there rose suddenly from the ships a tremendous "Hurrah!" It was our brothers greeting the dawn of freedom. And all of us who were not at the moment busy with the work of the ship rushed to the sides and responded with the same tremendous, joyous "Hurrah!" Caps flew into the water; with all our force we greeted the sailors and shouted to them to settle their officers.

But there was no initiative among them. . . . Meanwhile we had passed through the squadron, and were making for the open sea. The squadron stood still. We stood still also and, not caring to be cut off from our base, we backed towards Odessa. The squadron steamed to meet us. Again, we entered the circle, and again heard the tremendous "Hurrah!"

And the guns did their duty and, quietly menacing, shifted with the ships.

We were again on the Odessa side, and the squadron flying full steam away from us.

Was it possible that not one of the ironclads was going to join us?

But all at once we saw one ship, the *George the Victorious*, stand still and signal us by semaphore.

✶✶✶✶✶✶

Semaphore signalling is done in this way: on one ship a sailor moves two flags into various positions corresponding with the letters of the alphabet. The signalman on the other ship interprets them by means of a telescope.

✶✶✶✶✶✶

Our signalman interpreted. . . . I stood near him and heard him call the message out one word after another. . . . . As he spoke, the intervals between the words seemed to grow more and more insufferably long and tedious.

"The crew of the *George the Victorious*," he articulated slowly, watching through the telescope the rapid movements of the two flags on the *George*, "want to join. Beg *Potemkin* to come alongside." A shout of joy broke from all at once, when the signalman announced the request of the *George's* crew.

Again, I suggested to Alexeieff, who was standing near me, that we should immediately make for the *George*, arrest her officers, pursue the squadron at full steam, and capture it. But Alexeieff was afraid that the *George* had some treacherous design, that she would discharge her torpedoes at us, and so he refused to go alongside her. His terror for his own life, which the autocracy would be powerless to protect from the torpedoes aimed at us, led him to be careful of the safety of the *Potemkin*. Every time the *George* attempted to approach us, Alexeieff backed. Half an hour passed like this, and in that time the admiral, steaming at full pace away from us, succeeded in getting the squadron away from the infectious influence of the revolution.

Finally, we decided to send a torpedo-boat to the *George* with men authorised to arrest the officers. Kirill, Matushenko, and a sailor, K., went in the boat. I stood on the spar-deck beside Alexeieff and watched the torpedo-boat. She approached on the starboard side of the *George*, and several men from her went aboard the ship. For fifteen minutes there was no signal. Then from the torpedo-boat they signalled us to come alongside. But Alexeieff was even now unwilling. The *George* approached us: Alexeieff backed.

"So long as the officers of the *George* are on board, I won't let her come alongside us," Alexeieff said to me.

Then I resolved to go to the *George* to arrest the officers, and bring them to the *Potemkin*. An eight-oared boat was given me, and I set off. We were met half-way by a sloop with two sailors in it, one of whom brought a note saying:

The crew of the *George* will not decide on arresting officers. Send guard.

I rowed back at once to the *Potemkin* for a guard.

We had not long to wait. Sixteen men readily volunteered. That was enough, and again I was rowed off to the *George*. The boat flew swiftly along under the rhythmic strokes of the sturdy, practised oarsmen. The eight oars dropped evenly into the splashing waves. One more good pull and we reached the *George*.

"Guard, go on board," I commanded. The sailors ran nimbly up the ladder.

"Good-day to you, comrades," I said to the sailors of the *George*, who stood expecting us. "Where are your officers?"

"In the admiral's stateroom."

"Take us to them."

A sailor of the *George* led the way and we followed him with our rifles. At the stateroom a tragicomic scene took place. As soon as we were near, I commanded the guard to form. The sailors drew up in double file facing the stairs leading to the stateroom.

"March!" I commanded.

There was hesitation among the sailors; they stood in silence without moving. I understood them. To meet the enemy face to face is not hard, but to be struck down from behind a corner—from ambush, not seeing who is firing on you, and without a chance of parrying his attack—was very difficult, and it made even the bravest hesitate.

> Sailors, can terror have put such fetters on your hearts that they are not burning for revenge on your oppressors? can it have so fettered your hands that they cannot turn your bayonets against your tyrants? can it have so blinded your eyes that you don't see the sneers on the faces of the comrades you have asked to join you? How can they believe that you will fight fearlessly for freedom, when you are afraid of a handful of officers armed with revolvers? Don't let us cover ourselves with disgrace; let us go boldly forward.

So, saying, I led the way down the stairs. The sailors followed me. Slowly, holding our rifles at the ready, we went down. Suddenly, footsteps.... We were all alert, and there darted out to meet us—Kirill!

"Where are you going?"

"To arrest the officers."

"But they have been arrested already and disarmed."

We could not help smiling; all our fears and our fine words had been gratuitous. While we had been steeling our hearts to face death from the treacherous pistol-shots of the officers, the latter had been quietly packing up their belongings, and had not dreamed of having recourse to their weapons. The guard was simply wanted to take them to the *Potemkin*.

The officers finished their packing at last, and went up on deck. Matushenko, to whom I had handed over the command of the guard, gave the order, and they were instantly surrounded; then they were led to the ladder. When they were all seated in the sloop, the sailors of the George begged us not to kill any of them. We promised not to.

This request, as well as their reluctance to provide the guard for the arrest and escort of the officers betrayed the disinclination of the crew of the *George* to take on themselves any great responsibility.

The revolt of the *George* was due to the vigorous efforts of a few sailors, who saw the hesitating temper of the whole crew and their sympathy with the rising. They reversed the engines, and the crew was thrown into confusion. The squadron, steaming ahead at full speed, was by that time a long way off, and the *George* was nearer to us. On one side the crew saw the forces of the squadron removed to a distance, on the other side stood the *Potemkin*, which had thrown off the yoke hateful to the men of the *George*, and was ready to give them powerful support if they joined them, and to sink them if they tried to escape. And the crew of the *George* yielded under the pressure of this position.

All this, however, does not lessen the revolutionary significance of the adherence of the *George*, as the vigorous action of the few sailors of strong convictions could not have been successful without a general atmosphere of sympathy with the revolution.

But even while throwing in their lot with the *Potemkin*, the crew of the *George* instinctively tried to keep open a way of retreat for themselves by laying the responsibility for the mutiny on the men of the *Potemkin*. And we committed a great blunder in falling in with this desire on the part of the crew of the *George*,

Matushenko had left the ship with the officers. I remained behind on the *George*. Walking up and down on the deck and looking attentively at the sailors, I came across one "conductor," a man of somewhat squat figure, with a rather flattened nose, who excited in me a peculiar feeling of aversion. Cruelty, insolence and servility seemed all visible at once in his countenance. I was so much struck by his face that I went up to him at once and asked him what he wanted on a free ship. What was my amazement when I learned that he had been chosen by the men of the *George* as their commander? I inquired of the sailors at the time what motives had led them to elect him, and they explained that he was the one who thoroughly understood the navigation of the ship. But this choice of a commander was an omen of nothing good.

I don't know whether the men of the *George* were aware that I was not a sailor, but it was anyway evident to them that I was one of the leaders of the *Potemkin* men. A tall sailor with a bushy fair beard came up to me. His pale pock-marked face would have been ugly but for the expression of spiritual grandeur, which gave it a wonderful charm.

"My greetings and a petition to you, brother, and your sailors," he began. "I am, do you see, a Stundist, and do not approve the shedding of blood. Our religion forbids us to have any hand in it, and therefore we will not serve with arms; and we had troubles of all sorts till we were assigned the kitchen-work. So, see, brother, show us the grace of God; give us no other work. Leave us to the cooking."

"It's true, they don't approve of blood, because—it's the *shtunda*," the sailors standing round chimed in.

"Good," I answered; "if the government respected your convictions, be sure we will not do you violence. And now, brother, you do me a service: serve us some *borshtch*, for we have eaten nothing since morning."

The sailor K. standing by me seconded this request, and the gentle-hearted cook led us at once to the kitchen, set before us a mess of *borshtch*, and we sat down with several of the sailors and proceeded to demolish it to the accompaniment of the edifying discourse of the Stundist.

Meanwhile the *George* had followed the *Potemkin* to Odessa, and cast anchor at the entrance to the bay. When we had at last satisfied our ravenous appetites, we called the crew together and proceeded to the election of a committee. The sailor K. made an eloquent speech, explaining the importance of a committee, and urging the sailors to elect the men to form it. Names were shouted aloud, and for the most part approved by the crew. Several of the "conductors" were elected, and consented to serve on the committee. Suddenly one of them refused; at once the others, too, refused. This showed that the sailors had not grasped the real importance of the committee, and were exercising no special care in their selection of members. We proceeded to explain to the crew that only the men of the highest character, and of the greatest courage and devotion, should be chosen for the committee. When at last they realised this, the sailors cancelled their previous choice, and began electing new members.

The dusk of evening had fallen by the time we had finished with the organisation of the committee. The hour for prayer had come; the roll-call sounded, and the air was filled with harmonious singing. It was strange to hear the patriotic words of this prayer, here now, in a free ship, in the midst of the freedom of the sea. They were like a reminder that, though the old bogies were thrown down, their power was still unbroken.. ..

I was called away from these mournful reflections by the arrival of a cutter, sent by the controller of the port to the *George*. I rushed to the side of the ship, and asked the man in command of the cutter what he wanted.

"I am sent to you by the commander of the port to inquire whether the new ironclad is in need of anything," the man answered.

"Go to the flagship of the revolutionary squadron," I replied, pointing to the *Potemkin*; "the commander of the *George* is there, and he will inform you of our needs."

And the cutter of the *Tsar's* general returned to the menacing visitor to take instructions from it.

Meanwhile the evening prayer was over on the *George*, and the crew flocked to the admiral's room. I went there, too, and began to address them in a speech in which I tried to sketch the course of the Russian revolution up to the rising on the *Potemkin*, followed by that on the *George*. But I was interrupted in the middle of it by a sailor, who announced that they had sent for me to go to the *Potemkin*, as a torpedo-boat was on its way from the admiral to open negotiations.

I had to give up all idea of finishing my address to the men of the *George*, and K. and I, getting into the sloop, immediately set off for the *Potemkin*, There I learned that our crew, considering it dangerous to let the enemy's torpedo-boat come close, had sent a cutter to meet it and fetch the officer dispatched to us.

It was quite dark by now, and communication with the torpedo-boat was carried on by means of lights. All at once the latter began getting farther away, and soon disappeared altogether. The cutter returned and explained what had happened. It appeared that on the approach of the cutter the men in the torpedo-boat were frightened and, to their shame, took to flight, although they had been promised a safe conduct. So, it turned out that I had been fetched in such haste for nothing. I did not go back to the *George*, however, as we had to deliberate on a very important proposition, brought forward by one of our comrades belonging to the *George*, I believe, by Deiniga. (Deiniga, one of the most active leaders of the mutiny on the *George*, was condemned to death and shot at Sevastopol.)

He suggested that one half of the crew of the *George* should be transferred to the *Potemkin* and *vice versa*.

This proposition called forth many objections, chiefly based on the argument that in this way we should weaken the fighting capacity of both ships, as the sailors, not being at home in the ship, could not perform their duties so rapidly and so well in time of battle. It was therefore decided to transfer to the *George* only some sixty or seventy men, who could be dispensed with in action, and instructions were accordingly given to the superintendents of the various departments to make lists of the sailors whom they could spare for the *George*,

The committee proceeded to deal with various matters of trifling importance. I left them and began wandering about the ship.

It was by now night and perfectly dark. But the searchlights, working incessantly now on both the ironclads, broke up the darkness of the night. From each of the two ironclads there was thrown a broad track of light, and the searchlights cast their brilliant rays first in one direction and then in another. But sometimes the rays met and interlaced and danced together like careless water-witches, gaily sporting on the waves of the dark sea....

The sailors were all in good spirits, and chatting over their impressions of the day. All were in a fighting temper. They had seen the threatening squadron retreat before them without striking a blow, had seen the men who might have been expected to defend the old *régime* and to attack them show their full sympathy with them, and moreover, they had won a new force to their side. Now they were ready for the next determined action.

Wherever I went I heard excited talk.... But suddenly all were silent for a minute, when from the spar-deck where the man stood working the searchlight, we heard the terrible words: "A mine is floating here." Instantly there was a hush, then a brief bustle—the gunners rushing to the guns, and again a deathly stillness....

I ran to where the cutter was in readiness to go to meet the mine, and just had time to jump in as she put off. We set off to meet the horror. We all held our breath as though listening for it. There before us the rays of the searchlight showed us a patch of something white. We made straight for it.

It was coming nearer and nearer, and we were quieter and quieter in the cutter. We could hear our hearts beating.... Now we were quite close.... Suddenly we heard a merry laugh, and someone cried out: "Why, it's a wisp of straw!"

It actually was a bundle of straw, thrown overboard, probably, by some passing vessel.

Laughing at the terror aroused by such a foolish thing, we went back to the ship, where the gunners stood ready at the first signal from us to fire along the track thrown by the searchlight. Our news raised a laugh in the ship, too.

I went to the officer's room, and the sailors K. and Dymtchenko came to me there, and began telling me that it would be a good thing to send someone to the *George* to counteract the agitation being made there by the conservative part of the crew. I agreed with this and set off with K. for the *George*.

All was peace and stillness there. Almost all the crew were asleep, and only a few sailors were moving about the ship. One of these,

Deiniga, came up to me and began talking about the position of affairs. It was anything but reassuring; the crew were in a hesitating and apathetic mood, and the "conductors" and the commander were agitating for surrender.

We went to the admiral's room, and at the door I saw the commander in conversation with a sailor.

I pulled my revolver out of my pocket, and went up to him with a resolute air. "You are agitating for surrender?" I said. "Look here ... it's dangerous jesting with us. There would be no thinking twice about dropping you where the betrayers of the people have gone already. I advise you to do your duty honestly and conscientiously, or vengeance will not be long in coming."

But this man was made of different stuff from the officers, and showed far more self-possession and manliness. He answered me quietly and with dignity.

"Very well, if I don't please you, put me ashore. . . . No, with no 'if' about it," he added, with sudden resolution. "I beg you to put me ashore without delay."

I ought to have taken advantage of this request, to have called the committee together at once, and to have arranged to send him ashore. But I decided that it was too early to take steps which might excite the more ignorant part of the crew against us. And so, I told him that he would be sent ashore when we should think fit, and again warning him that he would be shot in case of disobedience, I went with K. and Deiniga to the admiral's room.

We fell to discussing the situation again. Vigorous and persistent agitation was essential; the whole of the next day would have to be spent in it.

And, meanwhile, we had not the strength for it. I was hopelessly hoarse after three days' almost incessant talking; Kirill was as bad, and Matushenko had almost entirely lost his voice. Fresh reinforcements were indispensable, and none had come from the town.

Making up our minds that on the morrow I should go to the town accompanied by armed sailors to fetch some more comrades, and laying our loaded revolvers beside us ready for any emergency, we fell into a dead sleep.

So, ended for me that eventful day, more eventful than the whole of my previous life. For in all my life I had not experienced so much rapture, and so much uncertainty as on that day.

CHAPTER 7
The Fourth Day

Waking at seven o'clock in the morning, I went out of the cabin with Kirill to find out whether all things were going well. It was an exquisite summer morning, and the smooth sea softly caressed the little squadron of our ships. In front of all stood the *Potemkin*; all about it were dotted our cutters and sloops; at a little distance lay the *Viekha*; and between the two giants a torpedo-boat basked in the sparkling sunshine.

Yes! already the revolution had a mighty force at her disposal. Her triumph was made sure, and the days of autocracy were numbered. On the morrow or the next day, we should take Odessa and arm the workmen, and then nothing could hold back the onrush of the people, in their wrath, with guns to support them. At one mighty stroke they would tear off their fetters and raze to the ground the whole edifice of oppression and tyranny.

My meditations were interrupted by the commander and some of the "conductors" of the *George*, again demanding to be set on shore.

I gave an evasive answer, and Kirill and I set off for the *Potemkin*,

I gazed with admiration at our beautiful, elegant ship, as we sped through the water towards her. I had begun to feel a love for the ship that now bore our hopes, mighty and proud as herself.

The sailors welcomed us with gay and friendly faces. We greeted them and went on to the officers' room, where a sitting of the committee took place at once. The temper of the men here was confident and determined. All were resting after the previous day's activity, and absorbed in considering the steps to be taken next. In such a mood they were not much cast down by the dispiriting news I brought from the *George*. The committee with unimpaired cheerfulness hoped to set it all right by energetic agitation. Kirill, Kovalenko, and Golenko were at once dispatched to the *George*, while I was commissioned to go to the town to fetch comrades to reinforce us.

The task before me was by no means an easy one. First of all, I had so to disguise myself as to escape being recognised by the soldiers and officers, who had seen me with the two deputations we had sent during the previous day. I spoke of this to the sailors, and some of them undertook to manage it. They set to work briskly, fetched a barber, hunted up some officer's shaving materials from a cabin, and in half an hour I was shaven and shorn.

A civilian dress had to be procured somehow, as I had given my suit to the sailor who had gone ashore with comrade A. They went off to make a quest among the sailors, and succeeded in getting a coat and waistcoat, boots, and a pair of immensely full trousers. As the latter were so hopelessly large, one of the sailors armed himself with thread and needle, and quickly rectified the defect. All this was accompanied with merry jokes full of true Russian humour.

When I went on deck the sailors did not recognise me, and stared in surprise at this new visitor.

A private sloop was somehow procured, and all was ready for our expedition.

We were just setting off, when Matushenko, who had been to the town to pay a thousand *roubles* for the wife of one of our officers, returned, bringing news which forced me to put off our visit for a while. He had made his way into the town, got as far as the Municipal Theatre, was there stopped and taken before a general. He had informed this gentleman of the object of his coming, and the general had offered to deliver the money for him; but Matushenko had been unwilling to trust him with it on his mere word, and asked for a receipt for the one thousand *roubles*.

What use the receipt was likely to be to him I don't know, but the high and mighty general promptly signed it for the humble sailor. I can fancy the anger in his noble heart when the latter told him he could not trust the word of an officer.

But the terror inspired by the *Potemkin* was such that the general swallowed his wrath and politely signed his name in token of the weakness and cowardice of the autocracy.

On his way back to the ship Matushenko met several soldiers, who urged him to begin bombarding the town again, promising to join the sailors. Matushenko, who had carefully observed the situation of the Nikolaevsky Boulevard, sketched a wonderfully correct plan of it, and proposed shelling the palace of the commander of the troops. This suggestion so fascinated us that we all became at once absorbed in discussing it. We were interrupted by our delegates returning from the *George*, accompanied by several sailors of that ship.

Their arrival brought us down sharply from the exultation of our bold projects to a much less attractive reality. It appeared that the position of affairs on the *George* was most unsatisfactory, that the "conductors" were openly urging the crew to go to Sevastopol and surrender, and half the crew were on their side. Our men were simply not allowed to speak; they were hissed and interrupted as soon as they attempted to address the crew.

Eager as we were to begin an attack on the town, we could not do so without making sure of the adherence of the *George* and creating a united feeling in her crew. We could not, without confident reliance on that united feeling, venture to open our attack on *Tsarism*. We saw clearly now the mistake we had made in not getting rid of the officers and "conductors." What could be expected of a soldier, who remained voluntarily in the service when his time of enforced bondage was over?

For his gay, careless existence he was indebted to *Tsarism!* It was his interest to maintain the autocracy. And for the most part the relations between the "conductors" and the sailors rested on nothing but force and the fist. Having risen from being mere sailors themselves, the "conductors" hated the sailors for reminding them of their past. Having been in a servile relation to the officers, these gentry, as such men always do, insisted on abject submission and servility from those beneath them; with rare exceptions they were brutal in their treatment of the sailors, and were devoted advocates of the fist and the lash. The sailors had not killed them at the time of the mutiny simply because they were men who had come originally from their own class.

We ought to have considered all this, and to have removed the "conductors" immediately on taking possession of the *George*, Not caring to risk offending the prejudices of the men, we did not venture to do so, even when their intrigues were apparent.

Now we saw the consequences of this blunder. The crew was already split into two parties, one of them openly antagonistic to us; the other was vacillating, and we could not reckon upon it. It was essential to correct our mistake by resolute measures before the disorganisation had gone farther still.

The committee determined, accordingly, to send at once to the *George* a deputation of several men accompanied by an armed guard to arrest the "conductors," and to bring them to the *Potemkin*, Some of our best speakers were to explain the meaning of this step, so as not to set the crew of the *George* against us.

But then the question arose: Who were to go to speak to the crew? Kirill refused point-blank, on account of the state of his voice, and Matushenko said the same. They were right, for they were so hoarse that they could hardly have addressed a crowd, and moreover an excited crowd. In the open air they could not have made themselves heard at all. Then Dr. Golenko, who had been speaking on the *George* against surrender already that morning, offered his services.

His offer helped to meet the difficulty, for though the doctor had no talent as an orator, his officer's uniform would carry some authority with the sailors, and we accepted him as one of the speakers, and fixed on two sailors to go with him. I resolved to go with him too, in spite of my hoarseness; but I was not ready, as it was out of the question to go to the *George* in the civilian disguise in which I had been dressed up. Begging the comrades to wait for me, I ran to the officers' wardroom, where I had left my sailor's uniform.

But Golenko was already bent on treachery, and my presence on the *George* did not fall in with his views at all. And so, when I ran out of the wardroom fifteen minutes later, I found the comrades had already set off for the *George*.

I ought to have followed them at once. But instead of that, I reflected that I really could hardly speak, as my voice utterly refused to serve me; that my presence would be useless; and that Dr. Golenko and the sailor Z. would be quite able to do what they had undertaken without me. I stayed . . . and committed a fearful sin—a sin that the long, sleepless nights in prison, that even the halter almost about my neck, can never expiate. It was a fearful, fatal blunder, amounting to a crime against the cause of the revolution, against my beloved country, against the comrades who had entrusted me with so great and glorious a task.. . ..

I stayed and watched the life of the ship, at this moment full of activity. A coal-barge had been towed up alongside, and coal was being loaded from her. All the sailors not on duty were merrily at work taking in the load of food for the huge belly of their "brave little ship," as Matushenko called it. The sailors, always so clean and smart in their handsome white shirts, an object of envy to the poor infantry soldiers, who stand a poor chance with the fair sex as soon as those white shirts come to outshine them, were now covered with a layer of coal dust. But this did not trouble them. Briskly and merrily they shouldered the great sacks and vanished with them into the yawning hold. And, just as merrily, dozens more kept running out like ants with empty sacks. I had never seen work so cheerfully and rapidly done.

It was by now four o'clock in the afternoon. The immense bay lay before us empty, but for the smoking tracks of two steamers. All the ships uninjured by the fire had left the bay, and were ranged in a picturesque circle in the harbour.

All of a sudden, a cutter came into sight on the deserted expanse of water. I was startled, thinking it was bringing me comrades from the Social Democrat organisations, and began to watch the cutter attentively. But instead of the red flag of the comrades I saw the white cockade of a servant of *Tsarism*. It turned out to be a cutter sent from the commander of the port to us with the provisions we had demanded on the previous day for our sick.

While the cutter was unloading, the officer in command, a red-nosed man with the typical Bourbon profile, came on board, and somehow found his way to the wardroom. Finding himself here in the respectable company of Alexeieff and the "conductors," he began holding forth on the theme of "autocracy, Orthodoxy, and Nationality." He had obviously been instructed by his superiors to investigate our state of mind, and, burning with zeal, the worthy man proceeded to utter his reflections upon the doings of the Jews. In his eagerness he quite forgot that there were on the ship "students," who in his little official mind were indistinguishable from Jews. He was the more painfully surprised by the treatment he received from Kirill, which was greeted by roars of laughter from the sailors.

The discomfited official beat a hasty retreat; and it was well he did, as a terrible moment was at hand—the treachery of the *George*.

We were all convinced that our deputation would be able to arrest the "conductors" and to bring the sailors of the *George* over to our side. And so, we calmly took in coal and went about our business. Our expectations would have been justified if we had not overlooked the fact that we had sent to work against the reaction an officer and a nobleman nursed and reared in the old *régime*, if we had not forgotten that in the French Revolution every adherent of that class was watched by the suspicious eye of the democracy, and a sword was always hanging over him, ready to strike him down at the first attempt at treachery. We paid cruelly for our oversight.

We had only just seen the champion of faith and patriotism depart, when a sailor ran in to Matushenko and me, telling us that a signal had been received from the *George* that she was lifting anchor and going to Sevastopol; she invited the crew of the *Potemkin* to follow her there. This news was so unexpected that we refused to believe it. The sailors, too, among whom it spread with lightning rapidity, would not credit it.

But soon the *George* forced us to believe it. She raised her anchor and began making for the open sea.

Such a decisive step in face of the menacing proximity of the *Potemkin* showed a reliance on the panic and disorganisation which the "conductors" of the *Potemkin* had doubtless guaranteed to introduce in the ranks of our sailors. This reliance proved to be well placed.

The treacherous act of the *George* moved our crew to indignation.

"What! They are betraying their comrades! They are going to surrender the ironclad to the autocracy! No, we won't give the ship up. We will teach these cursed cowards; we will manage the *George* ourselves; well work day and night, but we won't give the ironclad up.... Wait a bit, my lads, we'll show you—Sevastopol!"

This was how the sailors talked indignantly around us, while the *George* was steaming past us.

But no time was lost among us. Quickly the decks were cleared, the coal-barge was towed away, and when the war-alarm sounded every man was at his post. The guns were moving, and the menacing mouths turned and heaved till their fearful jaws gaped straight upon the traitor.

Another moment and another signal, and the *George* would be floundering under the fiery hail of our shells. But she was brought to her senses, and signalled: "I go back to place." Then she backed and returned to her former position.

The feeling of power and victory shone in our faces, while the *George*, humbled and vanquished, passed again by the ship which she had meant to leave alone in the struggle with *Tsarism*. Now she had reached her former position. But what was this? She did not come to a standstill there, but turned towards the bay. Before we could take in what she was doing, with one rush she was upon the mole in the middle of the harbour.

A terrible, critical moment had come, and something unexpected and awful had happened. Our position had become a dangerous one—dangerous because there was now a possibility of the *George* acting in common with the shore. Soldiers could be taken aboard now by the mole, and then the government would have at their disposal the very force that had been lacking.

On the other side the squadron, purged of revolutionary elements, might appear any day, and we should be between two fires. But rapid and resolute action on our part might have averted this danger. We ought at once to have dispatched a torpedo-boat to the ironclad to arrest the "conductors," to have set a guard of our men by the guns of the *George*, and then to have forced one of the steamers in the roads to tug the *George* off the mole, and by our guns to have prevented the junction of the ironclad with the forces on shore. The sailors of the *George* would not have dared to resist us in face of the overwhelming strength of the *Potemkin*.

But our leaders were inactive. . . .

Suddenly the cry arose: "To Roumania!" Someone took it up, then it spread farther, and in two minutes almost the whole crew were shouting the words as though bewitched. It was a moment of panic, provoked by the unexpected and dangerous turn of affairs. If the leaders had peremptorily and angrily ordered all the sailors to stand quietly at their posts, and then calm and authoritative instructions had been given them, the panic would have passed, and the ship would have been controlled again by disciplined and high-spirited men. But the officers were silent, and a band of sailors, previously enrolled in some secret organisation, and acting by concerted plan, ran about the ship spreading panic and crying: "To Roumania! to Roumania!"

I rushed up to the sailors standing on the spar-deck.

"Brothers, comrades! What are you about? You are ruining the cause—"

But I was not allowed to go on; several sailors ran up to me and, threatening me with their fists, shouted:

"What are you leading us into? What do you want? You want to see us drowned like sheep. Say another word, and well pitch you overboard."

"Silence, traitors!" I screamed at them, and I tried to go on speaking, but K. (one of the sailors) ran up to me and, drawing me aside, implored me not to go on talking.

"It's no use; you won't convince the crew now; you will only do for yourself and the cause too. Wait a bit; all is not lost yet. By tomorrow they will come to their senses, and then we'll turn things our way. If you go to work too directly, you'll ruin everything."

Not knowing what to do, I looked about me seeking some help and support. Suddenly I saw Matushenko. I ran to him with Kirill, who appeared all at once beside me. What was our amazement when we heard him, too, uttering those accursed words: "To Roumania!"

"Matushenko, only think," Kirill shouted to him, "we have six hundred workmen slaughtered in the port, on our conscience."

"What; are you in a funk, frightened for your skins? I can send you ashore if you like."

Matushenko, true to himself, had lost his head completely as soon as panic had taken possession of the mass.

And the panic grew and grew.... It was like some machine, gaining impetus and turning its wheels more and more rapidly....

Our cause was lost.... Orders were given already to get up steam, and the *Potemkin* was weighing anchor.

All at once I remembered our sailors and the doctor, who were onboard the *George*, and would fall into the hands of the authorities. The fearful thought of deserting our comrades fell on me like a thunderbolt, and I ran again to Murzak.

"The doctor and our sailors are there. We can't betray our comrades. Send a torpedo-boat for them."

"Yes; it has gone already. Yonder it goes," Murzak assured me. And, in fact, I saw a torpedo-boat approaching the *George*.

In spite of their panic, the sailors did not forget their comrades, and would not make their escape till they had saved them. And I imagine that if the crew of the *George* had refused to give up our comrades, the struggle would have broken out, the panic would have passed over, and the *Potemkin* would not have run away to Roumania.

I looked intently at the torpedo-boat and the treacherous *George*, which had so mercilessly ruined our plans. I was consumed by hatred for her, and if at one stroke I could have annihilated her at that moment, I should not have thought twice about doing it. I saw some dots running down the ladder and then running along the mole.

"That's our men running," someone shouted, and everyone heaved a sigh of relief.

The torpedo-boat went alongside and picked them up, and soon they were on board among us. I rushed to meet them, and only then observed the absence of the doctor.

"And the doctor? Where is he? Why have you left him? They'll hang him!"

"Hang? Not by his neck, but on his neck!" came the angry answer from Z., the sailor who had gone with him.

And he described the treacherous conduct of the doctor.

On arriving on board the *George*, Golenko at once informed the sailors that the *Potemkin* intended to surrender, and begged the *George* to go with her to Sevastopol; that only a few of her men wanted to fight, and that they were dominating the crew; that tomorrow, if not today, the sailors would throw off their yoke and make for Sevastopol.

Such a communication from the authorised representative of the *Potemkin* made an overwhelming impression on the crew. Z. made an attempt to reply, but the doctor and the "conductors" of the *George* would not let him speak. Things went on like this for two hours, and at last the doctor and the commander of the *George* together put the finishing touch to their manoeuvres. They suddenly gave the command to heave anchor, and as suddenly set the ship on the mole.

It was evident that a single organisation had been at work in all this on a preconcerted plan in both ships; and if we had formed a small compact group to resist this organisation, we could have succeeded in frustrating all their plans. But of that later.

A few minutes after the return of our comrades we weighed anchor and set off for Roumania.

It was hard to see the shores of Odessa retreating. What hopes, what bold plans we were leaving behind us there! . . . On those shores lay six hundred workmen, dead, slaughtered in that fearful night. Those bloodstained corpses seemed to stand on the shore, beseeching us to return to avenge them, threatening us with curses for betrayal and desertion. From that crowd of dead the figure of the young workman we had seen that morning on the steps pursued us, pointing to the bloodstained wound in his breast, and demanding vengeance, vengeance! . . . And behind him other figures seemed to be flying after us with curses on the base, treacherous fugitive. . . .

In terror, pursued by phantoms, I rushed to the wardroom. My mind worked in impotent misery and agitation.

To surrender without a blow at the moment when we were ready for battle, possessed of gigantic strength—at the moment when all Russia was hanging on our decision—seemed a fearful, unbearable disgrace which could not be outlived. . . . And the thought of death seemed near and sweet, bringing peace and settling fearful doubts.

I went up to Kirill. . . . His eyes were full of the same horror. . . .

I began to speak to him. There was no one in the wardroom but ourselves, and in the stillness there our despair found utterance.

"Yes, there is nothing else for us," said Kirill; "but we mustn't forget that we have to think of the cause first. Until we see that all is utterly lost, we must live and struggle on; and that's not clear yet."

And as though to confirm his words, Matushenko walked into the wardroom, quite his normal self again, and began assuring us that all was not lost even now, that the crew would think better of it, and that there was no reason for us to surrender in Roumania.

Encouraged by his words, we went up to the spar-deck. Odessa had by now completely disappeared from the horizon, and the great sea stretched on all sides around us. The *Potemkin* was flying towards other, foreign shores. What would they bring us? Was it to be the eternal, incredible disgrace of surrender?

Groups of sailors were standing about, eagerly engaged in discussing something. I went up to them, and found that in every group they were disputing about surrender. The better part of the crew had recovered their balance by now, and were passionately arguing against surrender. The rest were still obstinate; but it was evident that they were beginning to come over to the other side, and that by the time we reached Roumania the temper of the crew would be quite different.

My anticipations were justified sooner than I expected.

That same evening a crowded meeting of the committee was held to decide the question of surrender. Enthusiastic speeches and passionate appeals to continue the struggle were made, and all present were beginning to be affected by them, when K. came in, and, laying a cap full of money on the table, announced that all the sailors had given up their private money to the common purse of the whole crew.

This action of the crew, testifying to their zeal, decided the question, and the committee passed the resolution not to surrender in Roumania, but simply to ask for coal and provisions there. All felt as though they had wiped a stain off their conscience. Every face, till that moment uneasy and gloomy, beamed with satisfaction and relief. Only the "conductors" did not speak, and looked at us angrily. We could see that these gentlemen would not readily accept the decision of the crew, and were plotting something against us. . . .

When the committee meeting was over, I went up to Dymtchenko and told him of my apprehensions. Our rifles stood piled up in open pyramids, and the "conductors" could easily arm their adherents and kill the advanced and revolutionary part of the crew in the night. Everything, therefore, depended on the character of the men who formed the watch.

Dymtchenko agreed with me, and went at once to find the sailor who had charge of the watch for that day. He soon came back with him, and the latter reassured us, telling us that the watch consisted of the most trustworthy of the sailors.

So ended that day, that in the morning had promised us so much. In the morning we were masters of the position; in the morning we were hoping to join battle with *Tsarism*, and by evening to enter the town victorious.

In the evening . . . we were shamefully fleeing from the enemy, and afraid of being murdered in our sleep by a handful of the slaves of autocracy.

Chapter 8
Dorofy Koshuba

What though thou art dead! . . .
In the song of the brave
And the strong of heart
Thou art living on still
Proudly beckoning all
On to freedom, to light!
            Gorky: *Song of the Falcon.*

From the moment of the treachery of the *George* a new and powerful figure came to the front on the *Potemkin*—Dorofy Koshuba, comrade and hero.

There are men of such force, and at the same time of such bright, radiant personality, that the most skilful writer shrinks from any attempt to draw a portrait of them.

One who has stood very near the great man, and has passed through the greatest moments of his life at his side, must feel even more apprehensive of the task. A superfluous, misplaced touch may disfigure the picture of the hero and martyr, whose memory is sacred to him.

Great events give birth to great men, and often these giants spring from the most obscure surroundings. Fettered by the bondage of circumstance, they sleep in peace; but when the storm breaks, stirring up the muddy depths of life, the giant awakes, stretches his mighty limbs, and rises up in all his power and greatness. . . .

One of these giants roused by the hurricane of revolution was Koshuba. I can see him now as though he stood alive before me, a frail little man with ugly irregular features. Neither face nor figure gave a hint of the spiritual power hidden within. Only the keen little eyes showed the restless play of thought.

Till the *Potemkin* mutiny Koshuba had taken no part in political life; his immense vigour and energy had been wasted on trifling things. His active temper was quite unsuited to the narrow monotony of barrack life, and, finding no other outlet for his energies, he threw himself with intense eagerness into the study of naval work. But the brutal officers gave him a lesson that effectually turned him from that interest. When Koshuba, in his zeal, detected defects in the ship, and reported them to his superiors, he was thrown into prison; and Koshuba, seeing at last the stuff his officers were made of, realising the object our battleships are intended to serve, lost interest in working for their efficiency.

But his energies were seeking an outlet while the terrible conditions of Russian life prevented him from entering the party and throwing his strength and energy into the struggle for the freedom of the country that was so dear to him. He wasted his powers in petty feats of daring and gallantry among the sailors.

But at last the rifle-shots on board the *Potemkin* sent echoes into the sailors' barracks everywhere, and Koshuba was aroused.

With the daring, the fierceness, and the bloodthirstiness of a tiger towards the oppressor he joined a marvellous love and tenderness for the oppressed. He was an artist as well as a fighter. . . . He brought a wonderful poetry into every moment of the struggle. He drew such vivid pictures of the people in revolt, and the triumph of their victory, that everyone felt his heart involuntarily kindled, and a breath, now of death, now of happiness, seemed to float over all. . . . He was a poet of the struggle.

If Koshuba had not been in surroundings where talent is bound to waste away and perish, if he had not so soon been killed by the *Tsar's* butchers, the whole world might have caught the echoes of his marvellous songs, and all the oppressed—all that suffer under the yoke of despotism and of capital—might have been stirred up by them to struggle and revolt.

I first saw Koshuba on our ship after the desertion of the *George,* He managed to escape from the *George* with our delegates. He had hardly come on board the *Potemkin* before he made a passionate appeal to the sailors to punish the traitor *George*, and not to cover themselves with disgrace by surrender. A group of traitors prevented him from finishing his eloquent speech.

But Koshuba was not a man who could be forced by threats to give up a struggle. Soon after, in another part of the ship, his little figure was to be seen, transformed under the influence of the inspiration within. And again, he was drawing marvellous pictures one after another.

He had a new, wonderfully bold scheme to unfold.

This is what we'll do, brothers: we'll get up to within a hundred *versts* of Sevastopol, and will land a hundred determined fellows. They'll stuff their shirts full of cartridges, and by night fall upon the sentry and enter the town. They can make their way into the fortress unnoticed, giving themselves out for the government troops, arrest the officers there, and proclaim an insurrection.

Then followed a fearful picture of the people's vengeance on their tyrants, and a truly artistic description of the joy of the people at the arrival of the *Potemkin*—how all the suffering, all the oppressed, the whole Russian people, would come out to welcome it, and, climbing on to the roofs and tree-tops, would greet the eagerly looked-for ship with tears of rapture.

On all sides and at all times we could hear his gallant inspiring words.

Himself full of inexhaustible energy, he roused all, and let no one have a moment of forgetfulness.

I remember how once he put Kirill and me to shame in Theodosia. It was eight o'clock in the evening, and after eight days going hungry, we had just been served a hot meat supper. We were so exhausted, so worn out with those eight days of intense strain, with no meat and little food, and it was so snug and pleasant in the cabin, the soup smoked so appetizingly, that we could not help longing for half an hour's respite from that nervous tension, for a moment's forgetfulness.... And it was time to dispatch an ultimatum to the town about sending coal. But we yielded to our hunger and weariness, and resolved to see to this after supper.

All at once Koshuba ran in, and earnestly appealed to us:

What, comrades, you haven't dispatched the ultimatum, and you are sitting down to supper? Aren't you ashamed? Do you fancy if you drink a glass of vodka and eat a slice of meat, everything will then be all right, and the commander of the garrison will be touched by such a picture and let you have the coal? Or will you let our cause go for the sake of a glass of vodka?

Our faces grew red with shame at these simple words from the simple, untiring sailor. We got up abashed, and at once set to work to dispatch the ultimatum.

But Koshuba was not only great at rousing all the sailors to fight for the cause that was so dear to him. He knew how to fight himself, and was always the foremost in every enterprise. He always volunteered for the most dangerous exploits, and his face showed the keenest disappointment when, for any reason, his services were not accepted....

As soon as it was resolved at Theodosia to capture a vessel loaded with coal, he jumped into the cutter that was setting off to the port to make the attempt; and as soon as we came alongside the vessel, he was the first to leap aboard. He worked unceasingly at lifting the anchor, urging on the frightened sailors till the very moment when the first shots rang out. After a heroic attempt to reach the *Potemkin*, he was seized and taken to the fortress at the same time as I was. But arrest and the terror of the death penalty had no power to break the spirit of the hero. He persisted in his propaganda just as untiringly to the end.

In the presence of the officers he addressed the soldiers with passionate reproaches for firing at the sailors. While we were being conducted by *étape* to Sevastopol, he was persuading the soldiers of the escort never to consent to fire on the workmen. When we were taken to the sailors' quarters in Sevastopol, he appealed to the sailors to follow the example of the *Potemkin* men, and to kill all their officers. And on the *Pruth*, which was converted into a prison-ship, his was the only voice that rang out as bold and hearty as ever in the general panic that overtook the sailors. He alone succeeded in persuading the sailors not to betray their comrades, but to meet their doom calmly and with dignity.

Sleep in peace, dear comrade! Sleep, trusting that the triumph of the people's cause is near!

And you, sailors and soldiers, never forget the hero and martyr, the brave man who died at his post in the service of his country.

Chapter 9

The Fifth Day

The morning of the 18th of June found us in the broad, open sea. No coastline was in sight on the horizon; nothing could be seen but the free waves and the gambolling dolphins who followed us in shoals. Everything seemed full of freedom and gaiety, and the sailors' temper was in harmony with the day and the scene.

The crew had recovered their spirits, had determined not to surrender; everyone was light-hearted and contented. On the forecastle the sailors clustered in picturesque groups. In one they were playing the accordion, and a comical fellow, a petty officer called Zhuravlev, dressed up in a soldier's tunic and epaulettes, was acting a soldier. The sailors stood round, laughing merrily, and making jokes about the patches on the poor soldier's tunic. All at once they struck up the "*Kamarinskaia,*" and Zhuravlev fell to dancing. Several other sailors joined in, while the spectators clapped and chuckled with amusement. In another group the singers of the ship were singing a gay and rousing chorus. Kirill and I joined this group, and began teaching them some revolutionary songs. The sailors were delighted at this, and were soon singing in chorus, "Comrades, forward to the fight."

The broad and careless gallantry, regardless of the danger near at hand, the special recklessness of the Russian, were reflected in that gay, light-hearted crowd, doomed, in all likelihood, to a speedy death.

It was hard to believe that these were men who had entered upon a fearful conflict, who had been on short rations for five days past, and who were surrounded by dangers of all sorts. Only the day before we had learned from the captain of a ship coming from Sevastopol that the *Tsar* had commanded that we should be blown up, and that torpedoes had already been dispatched to carry out his orders. And all the sailors knew of this. But the news had not caused dismay; it had simply increased the spirit of anger among the sailors, and made them keep a sharper look-out for a wreath of smoke anywhere on the horizon.

So passed our journey to Roumania.

By four o'clock the coast of Roumania was sighted. First, we passed by an uninhabited island, called Snake Island, and then the coast itself came into sight. Everyone was excited at seeing it.

A committee meeting had been held in the morning to consider our position once more. Though the sailors were now against surrender, yet it might well be that if the Roumanian authorities were to suggest our surrendering, there would be vacillation among the sailors and the "conductors" would begin openly advocating it. We had to be prepared for this, and to have adequate arguments ready to meet it. Kirill, rummaging among the captain's books, had most appropriately made a discovery in a pamphlet on the regulations with regard to deserters. In every paragraph of this pamphlet he found it stated that deserters were liable to extradition, that by international law every government was bound to hand over deserters to their own government. Relying in the last extremity on this very weighty argument against surrender, we passed on to the consideration of other questions.

What were we going to do on reaching Roumania? Where should we go next? Refusing to surrender involved, as the only and inevitable course, continuing the conflict with the government. And the experience of these few days had shown us clearly that so long as we were not in close touch with the revolutionary workers, so long as the revolt at sea did not form part of the revolution on land, our cause could make no progress. It must therefore be our object to reach some place where we could be certain of rousing the people to insurrection at once.... The minds of all of us turned toward the Caucasus.

The revolutionary movement among the peasants and workmen of the Caucasus made their joining us a certainty. The revolution would take firm hold of all the Caucasus, would be impregnable in her mountain fastnesses, and might thence flow in spreading waves over all Russia.

Such were the conclusions reached in the morning in regard to our future action.

But, besides getting coal, we had another matter to think of in Roumania: that was to secure the sympathy of the public opinion of Western Europe. The most serious danger for us lay in the possibility of the intervention of other European rulers. The Russian government could not attack us. The other battleships would not turn their guns upon the *Potemkin*; there was not a man on them who would consent to fire on his brother-sailors. But considering the ambiguous position we were in as mutineers, and the reactionary character of certain European governments, the autocracy might, by putting our revolt in a certain light, secure the intervention of other European rulers. And before the overwhelming might of their fleets, which would certainly not hesitate to attack us, we could make no stand at all.

It was therefore essential for us to proclaim to the whole of Europe that we were not pirates, that we were fighting only against the autocracy, against barbarism—that we were fighting for progress and civilization. And so, we composed and printed two appeals: one addressed "to the whole civilized world"—that is, to the public opinion of Western Europe—the other a brief appeal to all the European monarchs.

Here is an exact copy of these two documents:

To the Whole Civilized World.

Citizens of all lands and of all nationalities! The grand spectacle of a great war for freedom is taking place before your eyes; the oppressed and enslaved Russian people has thrown off the yoke of ages and the tyranny of a despotic autocracy.

The ruin, the poverty, and the lawlessness to which the government has brought long-suffering Russia has filled full the cup of the patience of the labouring masses. In every town and hamlet, the fire of the people's fury and indignation has flamed up. The mighty cry from millions of Russian breasts, 'Away with the slavish chains of despotism, and hail to freedom!' has rolled like thunder over the boundless plains of Russia. But the *Tsar's* government has decreed it better to drown the country in the people's blood than to grant freedom and a better life. And the innocent blood of those who have sacrificed themselves in the fight has been poured out in floods over the whole land.

But the frantic government has forgotten one thing, that the army—in its darkness and oppression the powerful weapon of its bloody schemes—is the same people; that they are the sons of the labouring masses, who have sworn to win freedom. And sooner or later the army will understand and will refuse the shame of being butchers of their fathers and their brothers.

We, the crew of the battleship *Prince Potemkin Tavritchesky*, have resolutely and unanimously taken this first great step. May all those peasants and workmen, our brothers, who have fallen in the streets and fields of our fatherland by the bullets and bayonets of the soldiers, take their curse from off us now!

We are not their murderers; we are not the butchers of our own people, but their avengers. And our watchword is—'Death or freedom for the whole Russian people!'

We demand the immediate cessation of the senseless bloodshed on the fields of far Manchuria. We demand the convocation of an International Constituent Assembly on the basis of universal, direct, equal, and secret suffrage. For these demands we are all prepared to fight, and perish with our ship or conquer.

We firmly believe that the honest and working citizens of all lands and nationalities will be in the warmest sympathy with our great fight for freedom. Down with autocracy! And hurrah for the Parliament of the People!

Crew of the Squadron Ironclad '*Prince Potemkin Tavritchesky*,' and of torpedo-boat No. 267.

To all European Monarchs,

The crew of the squadron ironclad *Prince Potemkin Tavritchesky* has opened war upon the autocracy. While acquainting all European governments with this fact, we think it our duty to declare that we guarantee absolute security to all foreign vessels navigating in the Black Sea and all foreign ports situated therein.

Crew of the Squadron Ironclad *Prince Potemkin Tavritchesky*.

By these proclamations we tried to secure the support and assistance of the democracies of Western Europe against the reactionary propensities of their governments. And we resolved to act in the spirit of our proclamations. In Roumania we would not demand, but simply ask for, provisions.

And so, everything had been thought of and was in readiness when we reached the shores of Roumania. They were by now quite near. Soon the port of Constantia was in sight, and we cast anchor. At the same instant the signalman reported that some Roumanian officers were coming to us from the shore. Everyone rushed to starboard, and saw a cutter approaching, flying the Roumanian flag. A command rang out at once, and the guns boomed a salute, according to international custom, to the foreign power. The cutter had meanwhile reached the ladder, and two young Roumanian officers ascended it.

Kirill, Kovalenko, I, and a sailor who could speak Roumanian, went to meet them. Kovalenko informed them, through the sailor-interpreter, of the object of our presence there, and told them of the struggle we were carrying on. The officers were effusive in their praises of us. They declared that they, like all Europe, indeed, were in complete sympathy with us; that they looked on what we had done as a heroic exploit; that if they were Russians they would be in our ranks. But when it was a question of passing from words to deeds, these gentlemen showed a changed front at once. They would, of course, have been delighted to give us coal, but they must ask permission of their government first.

As if there were any regulation to prohibit giving coal to battleships without a permission from the government!

But didn't we want to surrender? They were convinced that their government would guarantee us security.

These gentlemen, who had just dubbed us heroes, imagined that we should be quite satisfied with having set people clacking about us, and now surrender would be no disgrace to us!

We made haste to refuse this honourable suggestion, and only begged them to communicate with Bucharest as quickly as possible. We also asked the officer in command of the port to authorise us to buy provisions for one day. That day we were spending in Roumania; consequently, this permission would not be helping us in our war with the autocracy, and Roumania would be committing no breach of neutrality in granting it.

The officer in command of the port agreed to this, and, taking our proclamations, promised to communicate them to the press, and to send them through the consuls to the various European governments. Then he returned to the shore, while the guns thundered another salute.

Before they left, the officers informed us that there was a Russian vessel stationed in the port, and asked us whether we wouldn't capture it. But we declined this amiable suggestion, as such an act threatened complications that might lead to foreign intervention. The echoes of the salute had hardly died away, however, when we were told by the men on the look-out in the conning-tower that the captain of the Russian vessel was approaching us in a sloop. In front of it our cutter was racing full sail to the ship.

Matushenko, who had set off to buy provisions ashore, on seeing the hated uniform of a Russian officer, was hurrying back to the ship to prepare a suitable reception for him. We ran up to Matushenko and tried to persuade him not to touch the officer, who was under the protection of the Roumanian flag. After a brief but heated altercation he agreed. Meanwhile the sloop came alongside; a guard of honour was drawn up, and the captain, covered with decorations, stepped to meet us with his report in his hand.

He was a short, rather stoutly-built man, with coarse and bloated features. His face became a wonderful picture of fury when Matushenko, Kirill, and I went up to him in our sailors' uniform and asked him what he wanted.

"How dare you speak to me like that? Where is your captain?"

This inquiry, coming from a man who had been in Europe, where the newspapers were full of news of the *Potemkin*, somewhat surprised us; but Matushenko answered coolly: "At the bottom of the sea." The captain's face changed, and he gasped.

"Is it possible that you don't know what has happened at home?" Kirill asked him.

"Why, no, brothers; I know nothing," faltered the captain. "I have been all the while on my ship, you know. We are stationed here to guard the Russian fishing-smacks. I don't read the papers, and I really don't know what has been happening."

Kirill began to tell him of the revolution in Russia, of the troops going over to the people's side, of the approaching end of the old *régime*. Kirill's impressive appearance, and still more the alarming nature of his information, made an overpowering impression on the poor fat man. He turned crimson and white by turns, and gasped helplessly, gazing at the sailors standing round. But, alas! there was no comfort for the frightened captain in those faces.

"So now, brothers, what are you going to do with us?" he asked, stuttering with terror, when Kirill had finished.

But when we simply asked him to leave the ship, the captain recovered a little.

"Well, well, brothers, goodbye. Wish you all good luck!"

And amidst the chuckles and jokes of the sailors, the captain went down the ladder. He was so unmanned that he went so far as to beg us to take him ashore in our sloop, as the sea was getting rougher, and it was risky to go ashore in his little sloop. Matushenko, who was starting again for the town to get provisions, had pity on him, and took him with him. . . .

Evening came on, and with it the question arose of the steps to be taken to guard against a night attack of torpedoes. It was absolutely necessary for the searchlight to watch the horizon. But we could not venture to use it without the sanction of the Roumanian authorities. A deputation was just starting for the town to ask for it, when the *Elizaveta*, a Roumanian cruiser anchored in the harbour, asked us to send deputies for negotiations.

Obviously, it was to discuss surrender. The committee assented, however, and chose me as a delegate. I got into the cutter, and we set off. Not knowing where the *Elizaveta*, was, we went in the direction of what looked like a dock. We were met on the way by a sloop, and heard a shout, "Where are you going?" in Russian. It turned out to be Matushenko. The cutter turned sharply and drew up alongside the sloop. The news he brought was bad. The Roumanians had some scheme afoot against us. Matushenko had gone into the town to buy provisions. He took a cab and told the man to drive to the market; but he began taking him somewhere else, and it was only with difficulty, threatening to shoot him, that Matushenko had induced him to stop, and then had gone on foot to the harbour.

It was quite probable that the Roumanian authorities were aiming at forcing us into some rash step which would provoke foreign intervention. What I knew of the reactionary character of the Roumanian government was quite in keeping with such a theory. That was how the sailors looked on the conduct of the Roumanians, and they were urgent with us to return to the ship. But Matushenko and I were resolved to hear the proposals of the Roumanian authorities; and, telling the sailors that we were going to the *Elizaveta*, we begged them not to take any serious step against Roumania if we were arrested. We decided that it was better for us two to fall into the hands of the Russian government than to risk the common cause.

Matushenko got into the cutter, and by his guidance we found the *Elizaveta*.

We found the Roumanian officers already at the ladder awaiting us. They invited us to go aboard. I wanted to go with Matushenko, but he suggested that I should stay on the cutter, the crew of which had been taken by a sudden panic, to prevent them from putting us to shame by making off at the critical moment. I consented, and Matushenko, after loading his revolver, went on board alone.

A quarter of an hour passed in agonising suspense, and Matushenko did not reappear. We were beginning to be excited, and I was just going to address the Roumanian sailors on the ladder, and to insist on Matushenko's returning immediately, when the latter himself appeared. We all gave a sigh of relief, and the swift cutter carried us back to our refuge, the ship.

Meanwhile a storm was blowing up. The wind whistled, and the breakers rose to meet us. The cutter rolled from side to side, but pushed proudly on, clearing the waves as they met it.

Our surmises proved correct. Matushenko was met on the *Elizaveta* by the same two officers and a general of some sort, and they all urged him with much eloquence to surrender. After hearing their arguments and their promises of personal security, Matushenko quietly replied that the ship did not belong to the sailors, but to the Russian people, and only to the Russian people could they surrender it.

This answer was not at all to the taste of the Roumanian authorities, and they cancelled the permission they had given for the purchase of provisions. They allowed the searchlight to work, however.

The searchlight, our tireless sentinel, was at once set going, and the gunners lay down by their guns without undressing. Had the torpedo-boats attempted to approach us, they would have quickly learned that the champions of the revolution were more vigilant than the officers of the autocracy, who could not with a whole system of searchlights ward off the attacks of the Japanese torpedoes.

The morning's dawn brought another question before us—where to go? The Roumanians had practically refused to grant what we asked for, and this forced us to make for some other place where we could obtain coal, provisions, and fresh water in sufficient quantity for our needs; for without all this we could not open a regular campaign against *Tsarism*. We could, indeed, hold out another week, by using the wooden decks for fuel, but that resource was only for the last extremity. We could use seawater in our boilers; but our boilers were coated with a thick layer of salt already, and were being ruined. Provisions, too, must be procured, as the crew had lived for the last seven days on nothing but bread and millet grain, and even these were running short.

And though the crew made no complaint, and did not put food forward as the foremost of their needs, the insufficiency of their rations sapped their energy. Only in Russia, where we could act freely, where we could reinforce our demands with the roar of cannon, could we obtain all we needed. And as there were in the Caucasus no great commercial ports where a large supply of coal would certainly be found, except the fortress of Batoum, which we could not venture to approach, we were forced to proceed first to some commercial port on the Black Sea coast, to take in a supply of coal and provisions, before going on to the Caucasus.

The committee met at five o'clock in the morning to consider the problem. All the men's faces were serious and thoughtful; there were none of the light-hearted jests we usually heard at the committee meetings. Everyone realised the importance of the question and the responsibility of advising on it, and each man was turning all his intelligence and his knowledge to the consideration of it.

The map of the coast lay unfolded on the table, and a chart of the Black Sea was brought in by the signalman.

First of all, everybody thought of Odessa, where the proletariat had supported us so splendidly. Immense numbers of coal-barges were always to be found in the port there, and it would be nothing for us to seize one of them. Kirill first put this idea into words, and urged us vigorously to go to Odessa. But I protested resolutely against the plan. The authorities in Odessa were by now prepared for our return there; by now they would have recovered from their first overwhelming shock, would have grown used to the idea of the *Potemkin*, and as soon as we left Roumania they would be looking out for us at Odessa. They might remove all the coal-ships, knowing we were in need of coal. Moreover, it was quite likely that mines had been laid by now in the roads, and we should be sent flying into the air before the people of Odessa could even hear of our coming. The authorities would guess how we must long to be back in Odessa, after the enthusiastic reception given to the *Potemkin* there.

No; we must go to a new port, and, taking the authorities by surprise, seize the stores we needed before they got over it. But in what port was there always an ample supply of coal? We invited the sailors who had special knowledge of the port to give their opinion on that point.

The squadron always shipped coal in the Gulf of Kertch; coal-steamers were continually passing out from it into the Black Sea, and several of the sailors suggested going to the gulf and seizing a Russian coal-barge by force. But an objection to this plan was that the Russian authorities, hearing from Roumania of our want of coal, and knowing that they could only seize us through this need, might close the Gulf of Kertch now, and not allow coal-ships to leave any of the ports of the Black Sea. (The fact that we did not meet any trading vessels on our return voyage in the Black Sea, which was usually teeming with them, confirmed this supposition.)

I dipped into the guide and read the list of Black Sea ports. Suddenly my eye was caught by the words:

Theodosia—commercial port.

I began reading at once, and saw that coal-vessels often put in at that port, and that there is a railway station. There must therefore be a large quantity of coal in one place from which we could procure it. At the same time, by going to Theodosia we should not be going far out of the way from our ultimate goal—the Caucasus.

I therefore immediately suggested the plan of going to Theodosia, and the committee proceeded to discuss it. Opinions were divided as to its merits. The chief opposition came from Kirill, who still urged us, as before, to go to Odessa.

I argued strongly against this.

Then a new person came forward—Alexeieff. He had till that moment preserved unbroken silence. Suddenly he began:

"Brothers," said he, "these two know nothing about it. We can't go to Odessa, for there are sure to be mines laid there; and there's never any coal in Theodosia. My advice is to go to Eupatoria. I know the coast of the Black Sea well, and I speak from experience when I say that Eupatoria's the only place where we can get coal. Believe me!

The wretch was plotting fresh treachery. Eupatoria, a little town with no trade except in sheep, had not even a harbour for ships. The passenger steamers of the Black Sea could not approach its shores, but had to anchor a mile and a half from the town. I knew the little town well, as I had spent a whole summer there, and I remembered that not one great ocean steamer had stopped there. Sailing schooners only, laden with sheep, traded from there to Turkey and towns on the Black Sea coast. There was no railway there either. But Eupatoria was only four hours' distance from Sevastopol, and Alexeieff was planning to bring us to that stronghold of the autocracy.

We did not understand his schemes then, as our minds were entirely absorbed with the question of coal. But I protested at once against his suggestion, proving that there was no store of coal at Eupatoria. I had no great trouble in doing so, for the sailors themselves knew that port well, and Alexeieff's schemes came to naught. Poor Alexeieff! He missed a masterly stroke for gaining the government favour!

After protracted discussion my plan was accepted, and it was decided to make for Theodosia immediately on receiving a final answer from the Roumanian authorities. Our decision was reached just in time, as a cutter from the officer in command of the port brought us straightway a formal refusal to let us have coal, and an invitation to send delegates to receive the king's telegram.

At first, we were unwilling even to go for this telegram; but on second thoughts we decided to submit everything to the scrutiny of the whole crew, and so sent Matushenko ashore. He soon returned, bringing the telegram, which urged us to surrender, and promised us security. The crew was assembled, and Matushenko, who had recovered his former fire, made a spirited speech against surrender. He said, in conclusion:

> Every country has its laws, its customs. But there is one feeling which all nations hold sacred—the feeling of responsibility to one's own country. Now, brothers, think a little how the Roumanian people will feel towards you when they learn that you have betrayed your country, and that, when you might have saved her from tyrants, you basely surrendered to save your skins. And what would your life be like here, when every Roumanian would meet you with contempt—when the children would point at you as traitors to your country, and the hatred

of all men would be about you?

These simple words went straight to the men's hearts, and had such effect that further discussion was unnecessary. The Roumanians' suggestion was declined, and we were soon moving away from their inhospitable shores.

Chapter 10
The Last Three Days

Again, like a phantom ship we were wandering over the open sea, which alone offered a refuge to the "red" ship, caressing it with her soft waves and singing it songs of freedom.

Evening was coming on when we left the shore, and soon we were hidden in the pitch-dark of a night full of dangers. We did not attempt to dispel that thick darkness with the rays of the searchlight, fearing to betray our whereabouts to the torpedo-boats that were hunting for us. There was not a light to be seen on the ship.

Only in the covered cabins and the machinery part there were lights, shining on the cheerful faces of the sailors.

Now we had said openly what no one had put directly into words before. Alone, unsupported by the squadron, we were entering on the real struggle with *Tsarism*. Now there was no room for hesitation; before us stood the alternative—to surrender under the protection of the Roumanian authorities or to enter on war to the death with *Tsarism*. We had chosen the latter.... And this terrible sense of the finality, the irrevocability of the position found expression in the resolution, passed immediately on leaving Roumania by the committee, to fly the red flag.

Though the sailors had, by the very fact of the mutiny, exchanged the flag of *Tsarism* for the red flag of revolution, still they had not come to the point of doing so formally. Many sentiments came into the question: the old superstitious reverence for the flag of St. Andrew, and the close association of the gallows with the red flag in their minds, and, perhaps, the sailors' dread of clearly and openly putting a name on their own action to themselves, of recognising the gulf which they had crossed.

All our efforts to haul down the St. Andrew's flag and to run up the red flag had been in vain; but now the position was so clear that our proposal was received with enthusiasm.

A committee was at once elected to make the flag. I don't remember who formed the committee, but I remember very well the inscriptions they put on the flag—"Liberty, Equality, and Fraternity" on one side, on the other "Long Live the Government of the People!" A big sheet of red cloth was pulled out, a painter was summoned, and soon the flag, painted in big white letters, hung drying in the wardroom. It was to be flying over the ship on its arrival at Theodosia.

It was resolved for that occasion to decorate the ship all over with flags, to show the inhabitants that we were not dreadful pirates, but friends and brothers coming to them; that we had not come to plunder the town, but to beg for help against the common foe.

With this object we resolved to invite the town representatives to come to us at once, to explain to them the object and character of our revolt, and to beg of them the requisite supply of coal and provisions. The whole of the following day we passed at sea. The ship, which was purposely kept at a low speed, so as to reach Theodosia by the morning of the next day, moved slowly through the vast expanse of waves.

Though the sea gave us a safe refuge, we began to feel our isolated position, cut off from all the world. The sailors had been in close touch with the workmen only on the first day of their stay at Odessa. After that fearful night of firing in Odessa, not a workman was to be seen on the shore; not a sloop came out to greet us. The town seemed as though dead, and the stillness of the tomb seemed all about us. It oppressed us; it seemed to tell us that now we were alone, engaged in a fearful duel. . . .

The thunder of our shells, the echoes of the "hurrahs" from the squadron, had broken that silence for a time, and filled the sailors with a sense of their own strength. Fearlessly they stood facing their merciless foe, until the treachery of their comrades put terror into their hearts and benumbed their faculties.

That terror and panic had passed, and their former courage had come back to them. In Roumania we had taken our stand, armed with all our old spirit and strength, and the suggestion of surrender was rejected unanimously.

The Roumanians had not given us the help that we needed. They had repulsed us without even a friendly greeting. . . .

And again we were alone in the vast expanse of sea, alone against the enemy, alone in the fearful conflict to come. . . .

The people, it is true, were ahead of us, but meanwhile we had no ally. . . .

And this isolation began to oppress us; it crept into the heart and filled it with dread and doubt. . . .

The boldest could easily struggle against it, but the weaker spirits were beginning to be overwhelmed by it; and the "conductors" were instilling fresh poison of doubt. In the hold, in dark corners of the ship, these poisonous snakes were sapping our cause at its roots. . . .

Matushenko caught one of them at it, and would have shot him on the spot. It would have been the truest wisdom; we ought to have inspired awe and terror in the hearts of the wretches who were pitilessly ruining the cause. . . . But we displayed, a stupid, senseless, criminal magnanimity. Criminal it was, for true is the saying of Isnar:

> In the cause of political freedom, to pardon a crime is to become an accomplice in it.

We pardoned them, and they persevered in their evil doing. . . . On the background of our isolation they wove the patterns of their imaginings; and at Theodosia they succeeded in outwitting us—at Theodosia, where there was no large working population, and where we could not receive an enthusiastic, encouraging welcome. There was another factor which sapped the spirits of the crew—the shortness of food and of coal. It was the eighth day since any of us had tasted meat. Bread, porridge, and water made up our entire diet, while we were every day expending an immense amount of nervous energy.

The condition of the engineers was particularly hard. They had to work in a fearful heat, to spend day and night in a burning hell. It was awful to see these harassed, exhausted men. I remember one day I went into the engine-room, and one of the machinists, a man called K., came up to me, and, his voice broken and gasping with fatigue, told me that working in summer-time in such heat, and on an empty stomach, was impossible. "We haven't the strength; our arms fall. Every moment you feel you will drop."

It needed all the self-sacrifice and devotion to the cause of these men to go on working in this hell. I only spent an hour there, and it was a long while before I got over the effects of the heat and jarring noise.

But besides the sailors' hunger, there was the still more terrible hunger of the ironclad. All the fresh water had long been finished. The distillery apparatus could not provide for more than the needs of the crew. Salt water had to be used for the boilers; but the salt rusted and clogged the pipes. And though Denisenko, the sailor in charge of the machinery department, allowed only some of the boilers to be in use at once, and kept cleaning the others; still, they were gradually being ruined. And the worst of it was that the "conductors" took advantage of this to spread rumours among the crew that the boilers would be unfit for use if we did not procure fresh water.

Coal, too, was running out, and there was only enough left to last, with the most rigid economy, for two or three days.

Still, though they may have weakened the fighting capacity of the ship, it was not the want of coal, nor the want of water, that forced the *Potemkin* to surrender. We could have held out a long time yet, and could, moreover, have obtained all we needed. But the "conductors," adroitly taking advantage of these defects and making them the basis of their agitation, spread rumours among the men that the ship would soon completely lose its fighting capacity, and be easily captured by the government.

These factors had more psychological than material influence in bringing about the surrender of the ship.

★★★★★★

We were all day long at sea, keeping a sharp look-out for a coal steamer. Not one vessel passed us except a Bulgarian battleship, which fired a salute to the ship of free Russia.

For one moment we had a glimpse in the distance of the snowy crests of the mountains of Caucasus. An exquisite view of the white mountain-tops, bathed in the clear blue ether, was unfolded for an instant, and then vanished.

And again we were alone—alone in the immense waste of waters. . . .

So, passed that day. The night we spent again in darkness.

★★★★★★

At dawn next day I waked, and got up to wander about the ship. The crew was up already, and a general clearing-up was going on. They were getting the ship ready for Theodosia. The gunners had taken the cases off the guns, and were rubbing up their brownish-black muzzles. The signalmen were hauling in ropes and hanging flags of different colours on them. The ship was decked up in holiday trim. Everything was bright and shining; and in these festive surroundings the faces of the sailors, too, were transformed, and looked radiant with cheerfulness and good-humour.

And now the shore came into sight, and the ship steamed at full speed. The red flag fluttered aloft, and the ship of freedom and revolution proudly cast anchor not far from the entrance to the Bay of

Theodosia.

Theodosia is a small trading-port, picturesquely placed at the foot of high mountains between the two fortresses Sevastopol and Kertch. The mountain heights that hem the little town in would have made it easy to hold against an enemy, and the smallness of the garrison—six hundred infantry without artillery—would have enabled us to capture it without much difficulty.

But in spite of this I protested warmly against the idea of seizing the town, a plan which Kirill brought forward that morning. There was in Theodosia hardly any industrial proletariat, so there would be no soldiers for the army of revolution. Of what elements could we create an army? Who would defend the town? At the same time Theodosia lay between two fortresses, which would throw all their armed forces upon the town; and how could it be defended? Where could guns be found when even the garrison here had none? To remain to defend the town would mean confining the revolution to one little corner, and so condemning it at once to failure. And to leave Theodosia to its fate, after the arrest of the authorities, would be an act of treachery to the inhabitants....

For these reasons we decided not to take Theodosia, but simply to procure there the supplies we needed.

As soon as we had anchored, our representatives, Kirill and two sailors, went ashore. Here they met with the same state of things as we had seen at Odessa. The inhabitants received them sympathetically, while the soldiers of the *Tsar*, always full of valour when facing an unarmed crowd, fled in panic at the sight of opponents with weapons.

The police not only abstained from arresting our representatives, but did not even venture to disperse the crowd, to which Kirill addressed fiery speeches.

After addressing the crowd, our delegates asked that the town representatives should come at once to the ship. A member of the local court, who was standing on the shore, promised to lay this request before the Town Council at once. Soon afterwards a cutter steamed out of the harbour to the *Potemkin*, and a few minutes later the representatives of the town were on board.

There were five of them: the mayor, a rather stoutly-built man; the clerk of the Town Council, a tall, keen man with clever and expressive eyes (I learned later that his name was Krym); his assistant, a fair man with a strikingly soft and winning face; an engineer of some sort (as I learned afterwards, the spy through whom we were subsequently caught in our attempt on the coal barge); and the town doctor, whom we had asked to visit our sick sailors.

After a brief greeting, they were conducted to the admiral's stateroom, where the whole committee was already assembled. One of us (I cannot recollect whether it was Kirill or Kovalenko) made a speech, saying that we were fighting for the freedom of all Russia, that our demand was for a Constituent Assembly—a demand that was now the rallying cry of all Russia. It was the duty of every citizen, of every public institution, to support us, by attracting the sympathy of the people to our side, by expounding the objects for which we were struggling, and also by the substantial assistance of providing us with the supplies we needed. We therefore appealed to the Theodosian municipal authorities to summon a meeting of the municipal council which would make known our political aims to the general public, and would provide us with the necessary supplies.

In his speech in reply Mr. Krym emphasized his sympathy with our demand for a Constituent Assembly, but added that he was opposed to election by direct suffrage of the people. Promising to carry out our requests, he asked what supplies we needed. Murzak furnished him with a list; it consisted of provisions, some articles needed for the machinery, coal, and water.

The municipal representatives agreed to furnish all these, except water, from the want of which they said the inhabitants were themselves suffering. After a little more conversation with us, they went away, promising to procure us everything by four o'clock.

It was by now eleven o'clock in the morning. The crew were about to sit down to their scanty dinner. Vodka was brought, and every sailor went up as usual to receive his glass. I went up, and then sat down to dinner with the sailors.

It was some time since I had dined with them, and now I regretted that I had not, for here the "conductors" carried on their agitation unobserved, and here one could get a true impression of the state of feeling in the crew. I found that down here the temper of the sailors was quite different from above on deck. Here I found a sort of uncertainty and depression in the men, and I realised that immediate and vigorous agitation was wanted; but for this we must have new men, as we two were not equal to dealing with all the tasks that fell to us already.

I had hardly gone up to the quarter-deck when I came upon Kirill, who had returned from the town bringing a government proclamation about the *Potemkin*. We resolved to use it as a means of agitation, and at once summoned the crew to a meeting.

The sun was baking hot, but no one regarded that. All listened with concentrated attention as Kirill read aloud the document. All was still, and his voice rang out so clearly that every sailor could hear him. . . . The stillness was only broken at times by comments or exclamations of indignation.

The falsity pervading the whole proclamation, and, above all, the promise to suppress the rising by strong and stern measures, enraged the sailors. As always, the government was the best advocate of revolution. Matushenko sprang at once on the capstan and made a fiery speech, then Dymtchenko and Koshuba, and finally Kirill, whose jokes had a wonderful success among the sailors, and kept them in roars of laughter.

Though the spirit of the crew was rising, there was not that powerful impulse which we had observed at Odessa after the bombardment and the arrival of the squadron. There seemed some sort of fear that we could not get at passing over the crew.

I had not time to address this meeting, as the signalman reported that there were people waving to us from the shore. Supposing that these were Social Democrat comrades, I decided to go to them to find out from them the exact position of affairs in the town, and to get some new comrades to join us on the ship. Koshuba and I, with Rieznetchenko, a splendid sailor, devoted to the cause, got into the sloop and went to the part of the beach where these persons were standing. The waves were high about our little boat, which was towed by the cutter, and dipped its bows every minute in the water.

But the shore was near; we could see the beach ahead, and the cutter heaved to. We unmoored our towing-line, and rowed to the beach. The short distance we had to row was very dangerous, as the breakers flung us every instant against the stones. Here, as always, Koshuba showed his devotion to the cause. He was all eagerness, looking intently at the shore, afraid the comrades would give us up and go away. He rowed vigorously, and kept urging the others to row faster. We were positively vexed with him, and began asking him to be quiet. Poor comrade! even his nearest friends did not realise his boundless love and devotion to the cause.

At last we were so near the beach that a workman on shore, taking off his boots and tucking up his enormously full trousers, waded out to us.

They turned out to be members of a workmen's organisation, unluckily quite ignorant, and unable even to give us the information we wanted. But they promised to take a message at once to the Social Democrats, asking them to send us some more comrades. Giving them the letters with which the sailors had entrusted us, we rowed back to the ship.

There we found the meeting over, and the sailors, prepared to unload a huge barque which had come alongside with supplies.

It was cheering to our empty stomachs to hear the lowing of oxen on it, to see the vast sacks of flour, of grain and potatoes, lying comfortably at the bottom of the barque, and the hens cackling, somewhat weary in their new surroundings in the midst of the sea.

The barque came alongside to port, the hatchways were opened, and the sailors set to work busily unloading her. They started first of all with the oxen. I watched curiously the deft and rapid process of loading. The oxen were tied up, and then a noose of rope fastened to the windlass was dropped a little below their forelegs. The word of command was shouted, and the beast was flying through the air. This was all done so quickly that before the bullock had time to bellow, he was on the main-deck.

As I stood watching the sailors busily at work, I noticed a sloop rowing towards us with two men in civilian dress in it. I ran to the ladder, hoping they were members of the Social Democrat society; but, alas! it was the town clerk and the correspondent of a French paper, who had come to ask permission to take photographs of the ship.

While he was engaged in doing so, the town clerk told me that the commanding officer of the garrison was preventing them from furnishing us with coal. This news sent Kirill off to the shore again to insist vigorously on getting the coal. But his menaces were all in vain. The authorities, who had received instructions telegraphed from St. Petersburg, refused point-blank to let us have coal. We sent delegates to them once more.

So, the day passed in fruitless negotiations.

By the evening it was clear that we should not get the coal that day. Precious time was being wasted, the enemy was gaining strength, and the spirit of the crew was sinking. Nothing but vigorous and determined action on our part could settle the matter. But seizing the coal by violence was difficult, from the circumstance that as far as we could learn there were no coal barges in the port, so that we should have had to take the town and to seize coal there. To do that we should have had to bombard the town, and so attack innocent people. This was what brought hesitation and division into the ranks of the most resolute sailors. There seemed no other course, however, and in the evening, we composed and sent to the Town Council the following ultimatum:

> If by six o'clock tomorrow morning coal has not been supplied, at ten o'clock the ironclad will open fire on the town. We beg to warn peaceable inhabitants.

Late in the evening I went up on the captain's bridge with Kovalenko. The night was calm on the sea. . . . A new moon had risen, and soon the full moon would make all the wiles of the *Tsar's* torpedoes harmless for us.

We began—I don't know why—to talk of the possibility of ruin being close upon us—a question that had never come up before, from want of time. We had had so much to do, and had been so absorbed, that we had literally not had the time to think of death, of danger. . . . But that night we began to talk of it, possibly because the government had held up the gallows to us today, by mentioning in the proclamation two students and officers who had taken part in the rising. But we were both cheerful and unshaken. Only once Kovalenko's gentle and honest face worked—when he spoke of his old mother and pictured her grief.

We talked a long while together. It was late when, warmly pressing each other's hands, we went down to the wardroom and flung ourselves, without undressing, into easy-chairs to sleep.

Neither of us dreamed when we said goodnight that it was the last time we should talk together on the "red" ship.

CHAPTER 11
How I Left the "Potemkin"

An astounding scene met our eyes at dawn next day—the flight of the inhabitants from the town. Women and children, young and old, walked, dragging bags and wallets on their backs; rich people in carriages were driving quickly in the midst of a crowd that looked like an ant-hill. This sight set our hearts aching, in spite of ourselves, at the thought that all the pitiful possessions of these poor wretches might be destroyed that day. But it was not the time for sympathetic feelings; the time was passing, and we had to learn the answer to our ultimatum.

Matushenko and I got into the cutter and set off for the shore. There the representative of the municipality was awaiting us already.

"No, the commanding officer refuses permission," he said abruptly.

"Wait till eleven o'clock; we have appealed to the governor, and are certain that he will allow us to give you the coal. For God's sake, wait!" he concluded imploringly.

We were faced by the alternative of refusing to spare the homes of the people of Theodosia or of risking the success of our movement by delay.

I chose the former, and answered the town representative accordingly, promising, however, to lay his request before the committee.

We were already on our way back to the ship when the idea occurred to me to explore the harbour and find out where there was coal stored. Matushenko agreed to the plan, and we steamed along the shore. What was our surprise and delight when we came upon three sailing-vessels, laden with some thirty thousand *poods* of excellent coal. The owner agreed to let us have the coal on condition that we towed the vessels to the ironclad ourselves.

We steamed back to the ship in a happy frame of mind. The difficulty was now solved in a very simple way, as under cover of a torpedo-boat it would be easy for the cutter to tow these vessels to the ship.

Quickly we selected fifteen men from the committee, and as quickly and, alas! light-heartedly, arranged the details of the expedition. Instead of assembling the crew and exacting an oath from them to defend us who were going for the coal, and then sounding the battle-alarm, so that in case of resistance on the part of the authorities every man would have been in his place and the guns would have given a menacing reply before the idea of flight could arise, we confined ourselves to manning the cutter with twenty-five determined sailors armed with rifles and ordering the torpedo-boat to follow us. This blunder arose from the excitement of our unexpected find, and also from the conviction that the soldiers would not fire on us, a conviction that brought the whole expedition to ruin.

It was arranged that the cutter should tow our vessel while the torpedo-boat, armed with small-calibre guns and manned by a crew of ten men, should protect us from attack by the troops. But here, too, we made a serious blunder; Matushenko, Koshuba, and I—that is, the most resolute of the party—all went in the cutter. We ought all to have been in the torpedo-boat, so as to force its crew to act at the critical moment.

All the men in the cutter were in excellent spirits no one doubted of the success of the undertaking, and the sailors positively laughed at those who loaded their rifles. They were so completely convinced that the soldiers would not fire! To those pure, awakening souls it was inconceivable that their brother-soldiers could fire on them. They firmly believed that the hour of the universal rising had come, and that the soldiers were only waiting for the signal to turn their weapons against the enemies of the people. ...

Cruelly they paid for their faith. . . .

When our cutter reached the vessel loaded with coal, all of us except a few sailors boarded it. We had to lift the anchor, and telling two or three men to keep a look-out on the shore, we set actively to work. The most vigorous of them all was Koshuba. I was hauling beside him, and marvelled at his iron energy. He hauled on untired, and when our arms were dropping with fatigue, with threats and entreaties he forced us to forget our weariness and to set to work again.

The anchor was rising higher and higher; in another moment it would be out of water and the vessel would be ours.

All at once a company of soldiers appeared on the shore, and before we had time to think what to do, we heard the crack of rifles, and two or three sailors dropped instantly into the water.

"Lads, take your rifles," shouted Mikishkin, a sailor, who was standing beside me. He snatched up his rifle and I seized mine, and we aimed them at the soldiers. But at that instant Mikishkin fell back with a bullet in his heart. I looked round—not one sailor; I glanced at the water, and there saw the dying eyes of Mikishkin, terrible, full of anguish, as it were beseeching for help. Beside myself, seeing nothing before me but those eyes, I plunged to his assistance. Clutching him, I swam towards the cutter. The soldiers had opened fire on the cutter, and to escape the bullets it was steaming away from us.

Bullets were dropping all round us, and the wounded and drowning sailors were struggling in the water. And the soldiers were firing in a sort of frenzy at the swimming and wounded men.

In the awful horror all round me, it did not occur to me to swim ashore, but I tried to overtake the cutter. But it was getting farther and farther away. When I reflected and turned to swim ashore, it was too late; my strength was exhausted, and I could scarcely keep up in the water.

The bullets were simply hailing about us. Suddenly one of them struck Mikishkin. He writhed convulsively. My tired hand lost hold of him, and he sank like a stone to the bottom. I dived at once, but could not catch him. . . . He was gone. . . . Somehow I managed to swim to a vessel that was moored close by, and caught hold of its iron anchor-chain. The murderous bullets were still dropping. . . . Holding on to the chain, I proceeded to undress. I held on like that for some time . . till the firing ceased.

The idea occurred to me to climb into the vessel by the chain. I began climbing up it . . . but my strength failed me, and when I had almost reached the top, I dropped like a stone into the water. Several times I tried again, but each time with the same result.

Then I heard something splash into the water not far from me. I looked round. Koshuba and another sailor called Zadorozhny had jumped into the water from the very ship from which we had been getting coal. The bullets had not touched them, and, waiting till the firing ceased, they had resolved to swim to the *Potemkin*.

"Where are you swimming?" I asked Koshuba.

"To the ironclad!"

"Swim, comrade, and tell the sailors that their murdered comrades cry for vengeance. Mind you get there, whatever danger you meet."

"All right," answered Koshuba, and he did his duty.

The soldiers, observing him, shouted to him to stop, threatening to fire, but he swam on. I heard the crack of a shot, the bullet grazed him slightly, but he swam on and on.

"Stop, or well kill you," the soldiers shouted to him again, but Koshuba, mindful of my injunction, swam on.

What happened to him later I did not see, as at that moment the soldiers observed me, and dragged me out of the water. But afterwards, in prison, Koshuba told me that the soldiers rowed after him in a sloop and picked him up.

I was quite numb by the time a soldier, walking along the shore, noticed me and sent a sloop for me. I lost consciousness, and dimly, as in a dream, I remember an officer asking whether I was wounded, a stretcher, and the green backs of men before me. . . .

When I came to myself, I was in the Red Cross tent. An army doctor was standing over me, giving me rum. An agreeable warmth ran through my body, and with pleasure I drank the revivifying spirit. But remembrance of the cold water sent a shiver through me.

"What's that, my lad? Don't be frightened," the doctor said kindly. "You're out of danger now; they won't do anything to you here."

I managed to explain that I was shivering with cold, not with terror. Then he ordered them to cover me up with great-coats. Snuggling comfortably under a warm, rough great-coat, I began to look about at my new surroundings.

I was lying in a big pavilion with a platform, and with long benches along the sides. What struck me most was the large supply of officers here. There were twelve of them. One would have supposed that now that a battle was expected they ought to have been at their posts. Or was this the headquarters of the staff?

A young officer set my doubts at rest. Coming up to me, he asked in an ingratiating voice: "I say, sailor, they won't fire at this tent from the ironclad, will they? There's the Red Cross flag flying here, you know."

"How will it be seen from there?" I answered. The officer started and exchanged glances with another officer.

The gallant company of officers were in hiding in the Red Cross tent, seeking safety under its flag from the avenging shells of the battleship.

The officers were beginning to address me on some other subject, but at that moment another sailor was brought in on a stretcher.

"Wounded?" asked the doctor, running up to him.

"Not at all, your honour."

I stared intently at this group in the hope of seeing Koshuba there. But it turned out to be Zadorozhny, who had been picked up in the harbour.

I had quite come to myself, and was sitting on a bench. They made Zadorozhny sit beside me.

"Well, what will happen now?" I asked him.

"Why, they'll go to Roumania to surrender! That's as sure as God is holy."

And his answer proved that an agitation in favour of surrender had been going on already in the lower ranks of the crew, and the "conductors" had formed a strong organisation.

The entrance of another stretcher interrupted my meditations.

"Wounded," shouted the soldiers.

"Koshuba," flashed through my head, and I was rushing to him. But they made me sit down where I was before.

"Oh, it's a trifle," said the doctor; "he'll be all right directly." And Koshuba did, in fact, come to himself very soon, and he got up and sat down with us. The officers were amazingly amiable to us. Hearing that we were hungry, they ordered tea and an omelet to be brought us. They advised us how to behave at the examination, asked whether there were any officers on board, and suggested that we should surrender. When we refused, the officers seemed surprised, and one of them, a captain, who had come back from Port Arthur, even expressed a desire to ask leave of the officer in command of the garrison to go on board the *Potemkin*, and persuade the sailors to surrender. But I made haste to assure him of the hopelessness of such an attempt. The amiable behaviour of the officers to us lasted till the moment when the *Potemkin* disappeared from the horizon. The terror of the coming vengeance of the sailors led these cowards to flatter and sympathize with us.

But the behaviour of Gertsyk, the officer in command of the garrison, was a sharply discordant note in the sympathetic chorus. On entering the tent for a few moments and seeing us, Gertsyk flew into such a violent fury that he positively could not speak. He shook his fists furiously at us, threatened us with the gallows, and uttered disconnected inarticulate noises. At last, having satisfied his feelings, he went away.

We were led out into a sunny garden walk. It was warm and pleasant in the sun, and for a minute I forgot everything as my chilled limbs basked in the hot sunshine.

All of a sudden, a man in civilian dress walked into the garden and began to approach us. Looking more closely at him, I recognised Krym, the member of the local court, who had been on the ironclad the previous day.

"Tell me, gentlemen, are they going to fire from the ironclad?" he asked us. "I must know, so as to warn the inhabitants. Pillaging has begun in the town already."

I answered that I did not know, and advised him to go to the ironclad and inquire of the sailors. He agreed, and walked away. My heart thrilled with excitement. Perhaps he would tell the sailors we were not killed, and they would bombard the town, and demand our release. I longed to be with them, if only for a moment. I would have told them how their brothers had died; I would have told them so that the hearts of the feeblest, of the cowardliest, would have turned with hatred and desire of revenge.

But I was not kept long in suspense. Before Krym reached the garden gate, a horseman galloped up and uttered the fatal words:

The ironclad has disappeared from the horizon . . . .

CHAPTER 12
Conclusion

Three days later I learned from the soldiers who were in charge of me that the *Potemkin* had surrendered, and three months later, when I was living abroad, I heard from Kirill the details of the panic on the ship, which was caused by the soldiers firing, and led the *Potemkin* to steam for Roumania to surrender.

In general outline, it was the same story over again as the panic on the desertion of the *George*, At the unexpected blow the crew were seized with panic; the men in charge of the mines and engines—the picked men of the crew—rushed to their several departments; the nominal leaders were inactive. . . , Again someone shouted: "To Roumania!" . . . Again sailors, unnoticed till then, ran up and down the deck increasing the panic. . . . Again, Kirill appealed to Matushenko, and again he was told that he was a landsman, and knew nothing about it.

The only difference was that this time the more advanced part of the crew hesitated also, being unwilling to shell the houses of peaceable citizens. The splendid, mighty fortress surrendered in full fighting trim. . . .

It was only later on, when I was free, and the first horror and nightmare of that surrender had passed, that I could reflect coolly and objectively on the causes of the failure of our plans. And analysing all that had happened, I saw that the chief cause, by which our rising was doomed to failure, lay outside ourselves: it lay in the *insufficient development of the revolution on the shore.*

Could we really have been victorious while all the surrounding coast of Russia took so passive an attitude to our rising? Why did the workmen make no sign in the neighbouring towns from which troops were drafted to Odessa? Why didn't they tear up the railway-lines, break down the bridges, and isolate the authorities in Odessa? Why did not the peasants of the surrounding district send detachments of their sons to the aid of the workmen in Odessa?

Because they were not sufficiently prepared for the revolution!

And if that were so, we could not by ourselves, by our own forces alone, have vanquished a monstrous growth of the ages like *Tsarism*.

"But you didn't even attempt to vanquish it," I shall be told. "Did you make an effort to take the town? Surely it wasn't because you were afraid of not being a match for the troops there that you could not venture to attempt it? And if so, wasn't it all the same to you whether they were few or many?"

Yes, that is true. We did not even venture on beginning a real struggle with *Tsarism*. But does not the very fact of that hesitation confirm my idea? We did not dare because the shore made no sign.

The unreflecting mass of men on the *Potemkin*, who had only just broken with the old order of things, did not dare to act alone against *Tsarism*. Instinctively they sought an ally. . . . Their eyes turned to the squadron, because they saw in it a substantial force.

Did this mean that the people, too, must have been relying entirely on the squadron? Ought they not, on the contrary, by displaying the utmost revolutionary energy, to have shown the *Potemkin* men that they must look to them, the working people, as their powerful and trustworthy allies?

If the sailors had heard that the workmen were tearing up the railway-lines to hinder the forwarding of troops, that companies of peasants and workmen were moving from all parts to the assistance of the rising, that the workmen were forging weapons in the foundries; if the working-classes of Odessa, who held the port the first day of the *Potemkin*'s presence there, had refused to leave it, and, regardless of the sailors' reluctance to bombard the town, had barricaded themselves there; in short, if the people on the shore had not *waited*, but *fought*, then the sailors would have rushed to their aid, without waiting for the squadron. They would have hurried to support them, because the sailors could not have looked with unconcern at their brothers suffering in a bloody strife. At the time of the fire at Odessa the sailors had wanted to go ashore to stop the firing of the soldiers.

On shore they waited for a signal from the *Potemkin*. Remember what the representatives of the Social Democrat organisations said to the workmen when they were assembled on the shore. They urged the men to go quietly to their homes, and not to make any attempt till the *Potemkin* took action.

The workmen went home.

More and more troops kept passing into the town. The sailors saw the power of the government continually growing in Odessa, and felt at the same time that they had no active and powerful support there.

Still more strongly they felt that it was only from the squadron that they could get the support of overwhelming force. And they waited for the squadron.

The *George* deserted them and the last hope of help from the squadron crumbled away. The sense of their isolation came upon the sailors, troubled their spirits, and helped the "conductors" to achieve their plan of flight to Roumania. The most favourable moment for the rising was lost. Those first days when, owing to the panic of the authorities and the wavering of the troops, we might easily have taken the town, we did nothing; and our passivity was to a great extent the cause of our isolation. And later on, this factor was even more strongly felt.

There were, of course, in the ship, too, grave defects which were largely responsible for our inactivity and surrender. The most terrible defect was that in critical moments the control lay in feeble hands. If the reader recalls the account of the approach of the squadron and of the desertion of the *George*, it will be clear to him how largely this circumstance was to blame for our failure.

A serious blunder was made by us—Kirill, A., and me—in not forming a compact group of the more determined men to counteract the secret intrigues of the "conductors." The reader will probably remember that the reactionists acted on a preconcerted plan, that they were successful because the revolutionary party in the crew was not organised in the same way, but was, on the contrary, entirely disorganised. The best men were at critical moments always in the machinery part of the ship, and the handful of resolute men left on deck, where the fate of the rising was determined, were scattered and acted on no settled plan. Had there been some thirty or forty determined men, obeying a central authority, had they snatched up their rifles and threatened with death anyone who increased the panic among the sailors, and called a meeting of the whole crew, then the crew might still have been kept in hand.

But afraid of bringing dissension into the crew, afraid of looking the position straight in the face, we did not do this. The limited propaganda we were able to carry on, owing to being so few, allowing the "conductors" to remain, and a whole host of other blunders on our part, all worked together against the success of the rising.

It was not cowardice and panic that led the sailors of the *Potemkin* to surrender. There were a number of causes leading to the surrender, that lay outside them.

And if anyone cares to get a true idea of the influence of those forces, he must remember that the sailors of the *Potemkin* were by no means exceptional men, such as might be unmoved by their surrounding conditions; he must remember that, brave and devoted as they were, they had not at the time of the mutiny that profound understanding of the revolution, and that faith in its ultimate triumph, which enables men to go boldly and resolutely forward, to persist without faltering in the work they have begun. He must remember that they were the first soldiers entering on the path of revolution, and that they had no previous experience to show them that they were not alone, that all the navy and the army were in the opposition now.

And tragic as the issue of this rising was, it was none the less a great moment in the Russian revolution.

It is enough to recall the mutinies of marines and of soldiers that followed, to realise the part played by the *Potemkin* in the great world tragedy—the Russian revolution.

Chapter 13
My Escape from Prison

The ironclad has disappeared from the horizon!

This sentence echoed with agonising pain in my heart. All at once all the strength and brightness that we had been living in during those days had been torn away, and a boundless dejection fell upon me and set my heart aching. . . . Everything around me was in keeping with it; a death-like stillness reigned in the deserted town; the soldiers and officers, impressed by the drama that had just passed before their eyes were sullenly silent. . . . What called forth this depression? Was it the desertion of the comrades who had left us in the hands of the government or a vague conviction of the surrender that would follow. . I can't tell. To this day I am unable to analyse the suffering I experienced then. Mournfully I remembered how the torpedo-boat had made off at the critical moment, not even picking up the wounded comrades. . . . But what fretted me most of all was the uncertainty as to the future doings of the *Potemkin*.

I thought of the depressed mood of the crew, of Zadorozhny's ominous words of flight to Roumania. All this I put together with the want of coal and the departure from Theodosia . . . and I could not help a doubt creeping into my mind, while the idea that such a splendid exploit could end in surrender was an agony to me. . . .

Which way had the ship gone? East or west? To fight or to surrender? If only to the east! Then I could forgive the sailors their flight and their desertion. . . . My arrest itself did not terrify me; those days had trained us to stand face to face with death, and I could look forward without flinching. I felt strength within to struggle in the very clutches of *Tsarism*, and the thought of the trial, at which I could succeed in exposing to the whole world the feebleness of the autocracy alternated with the thought of escape. Till the day of the trial I resolved to do my utmost to escape from the butchers' hands.

My thoughts passed soon to the practical means of achieving this. First of all, I must take up the pose that would be most likely to promote my chances of escape. ... I knew very well that I should be looked after a great deal more strictly if I were discovered to be a civilian, and I therefore resolved to give myself out as a sailor. But a few hours later, through betrayal, and the experience of the *gendarmes*, my true character was disclosed.

Soon after the departure of the *Potemkin*, two *gendarme* officers appeared at the garden gate, and came towards us with a confident and authoritative air. The officer in charge of us made an attempt to prevent their entering, but the colonel of *gendarmes* shouted gruffly to him and came up to me.

"A sailor?"

"Yes, please your honour."

"Of what class?"

"First class, your honour."

"Show your hands. Well, you're a pretty sailor," the colonel commented, looking at my outstretched hands, free from any trace of hard manual work.

"What's your name?"

"Fyodor Mikishkin."

"Take down his name," said the colonel to the officer accompanying him, "and telegraph at once to Sevastopol to inquire if there is such a sailor."

The *gendarmes* passed to Koshuba. For some reason Koshuba at first did not give his own name.

"Well, are you sorry for all the harm you have done?" the colonel asked of Ivan Zadorozhny.

"What is there to be sorry for? We have done nothing wrong," Zadorozhny, a good-hearted Little Russian, answered simply and coolly.

"Oh, very well! When you come into my hands, then you'll be sorry!"

But the colonel's good wishes were not destined to be carried out, as almost at that moment a company of soldiers came in at the gate with instructions from Gertsyk, the commander of the garrison, to conduct us to the military guard-house. Forming the company into a circle, the officer put us in the middle of it, and led us through the absolutely deserted streets. It was only when we were near the guard-house a crowd of workmen and workwomen appeared and walked behind us.... Their faces showed sympathy and readiness to help us.. ... But ... the bayonets glittered....

In the guard-house we found six more sailors who had been

caught. With them was a seventh, a sailor who had swum ashore from the *Potemkin* on the previous night, to give himself up to the authorities. On seeing me, he cried out: "Why, there's our student!" In this way my position was at once discovered. . . .

We were put in solitary, dark, damp cells, the windows of which were closed fast with heavy shutters. Light and air could only penetrate to the cell through a little hole in the doors, which opened into a filthy corridor.

★★★★★★★★★★

A few days after we had been shut up, a little Jewish soldier came to the door of my cell. Telling me his name was Moshedlober, and he was a drummer, he began saying how bitter and intolerable the thought of the soldiers having fired on the sailors was to him.

"I can't keep quiet, I must protest!" he concluded his nervous speech. And on the spot, he offered me his assistance to escape.

The circumstances were fairly favourable. The window of my cell looked into the street, where there was no sentinel posted. It was so low that anyone could easily from the street file through the grating and set me free.

Koshuba's escape could be managed in the same way.

Moshedlober undertook to arrange it all that very night.

A few hours later he shot at Gertsyk. The soldiers told us that when Gertsyk was inspecting them, he began praising them for the gallant way they had fired on the sailors. And the anger and resentment which had been rankling for days in Moshedlober's heart against the butcher broke out at his insolent, cynical words. He snatched a rifle from a soldier near him, and fired two shots at Gertsyk. But through the violent excitement natural in such a sudden outbreak, he missed his aim, and an innocent soldier fell a victim of his holy vengeance. Within a month he was executed. . . . So perished that pure heart, that knew not how to bear the mocking cruelty of the oppressors. . . .

With Moshedlober's arrest all hope of escape from the guardhouse in Theodosia vanished, as I was transferred the same day to a cell the window of which looked into the courtyard of the guardhouse where there was a whole company of soldiers stationed. Sentinels were posted all round the building. The guard, which had numbered under thirty men, was increased now to two companies.

This increased supervision was the result, so an officer told me, of instructions telegraphed by Tchuhnin. It was kept up all the while we were in the guard-house, and was greatly resented by the soldiers, who, apart from this, were already exasperated against their officers. The unrelieved, objectless sentry-duty in the heat of summer seemed to make them feel as though they were not in Russia, but in some hostile country.

"As though we were in the Japanese war," they said to one another.

Often, they came up to our windows and asked us to tell them how we had killed our officers.

And as we explained what we were struggling for and against, their faces grew keener, and more and more of them gathered round our windows.

"It's the truth, lads, the sailors are speaking," one would exclaim, "and we ought to have done the same long ago! The only thing is. . . *Ekh!* we're not men! . . ."

Sometimes there was even a discussion of the plan of revolt; the chief obstacle lay in the distrust of the other parts of the army.

"It was easy for you to begin; you were shut up in a battleship; you had a force and a fortress. . . . There, whether others back you or not, you can hold your own. But with us, if one company rises and comes out with their rifles, there would be ten companies against it. And, too, while our cartridges last, it's all right; but when we had fired them all, we'd be killed like chickens," said the soldiers.

"Don't be downhearted though, maybe we'll get you out yet," they would wind up, trying to cheer us.

Only the soldiers of the seventh and ninth companies, those which had fired on us, maintained an angry and sullen silence when they were on duty. Their behaviour was really due less to hostility than to shame, which they felt the more keenly from the other soldiers boycotting them.

The officers of the Theodosia garrison were very different indeed. They used often to visit the guardhouse and to talk to the sailors and soldiers. And there was such a spirit of savage inhumanity in their words that sometimes it gave me a feeling of horror at the possibilities of human nature.

One night I waked up at a noise, and saw two officers in my cell. One of them I recognised as a lieutenant of the garrison, the other, a smart *gendarme* officer, I saw for the first time.

"Your Christian and surname," the latter said to me, as soon as he noticed that I was awake.

"That does not concern you," I answered, completely waking up and realising it was a night visit of the *gendarmes*; "but can I not be spared visitations at night?"

"Pardon me," said the officer, with typically *gendarme* politeness, "but I have only just arrived from St. Petersburg, and I have to go back at once. So why won't you tell us your name? You will be found out, you know, anyway. And at the very last you won't deny your identity, I hope?"

"Most likely!"

"There's a strange logic in all revolutionists. Here Kalyaev—would you believe it?—said just the same to me, but when he was identified, he acknowledged his name. Does it matter to you whether we find you out an hour sooner or later?"

"Allow me to judge of that myself."

"Perhaps you will reconsider it? I will stay till tomorrow."

"As you please."

"*Monsieur le capitaine* is very busy," Pomerantsev, the lieutenant, said suddenly. "Tell us, will you perhaps change your mind tomorrow; then he will stay?"

"I imagine that it would be useless."

The officers retired. But still the captain of *gendarmerie* came again to see me next day, and did his utmost to find out my name.

From that day Pomerantsev made it his object to find out my name, and what part I had taken in the revolt. He used to come to the sailors and try every means to persuade them to tell him my name.

"If you tell his name, lads, you will get no harm. And he's a Jew, why waste your pity on him? If you won't tell, it will go badly with you; you'll all be hanged!"

But alas! all the eloquence of this volunteer detective was doomed to failure from the simple fact that not one of the sailors knew my name.

Another favourite pursuit of Lieutenant Pomerantsev and the other officers was inciting the soldiers to *pogrom* activity. I remember his coming one evening to the guard-house and talking to the soldiers about Moshedlober's act.

"What, lads, do you suppose he killed the soldier by accident? A fellow like that? And all the disturbance they're making on account of this Jew! You beat them, cut them to pieces, stick them with your bayonets! You may be sure you won't get into trouble. As soon as one of them kills a Christian, you run out into the street and kill all the Jews!"

Gertsyk himself said something not very different.

Such were the officers at Theodosia.

****

On the fourth day of our stay in the guard-house we learned from the newspaper that the *Potemkin* had surrendered.

If the reader remembers the proud and bold hopes in which we lived on the *Potemkin*, he will be able to imagine how we felt at the news of the surrender.

At the time I could not analyse clearly the causes of the surrender ... and it seemed to me a betrayal of our country's cause, a fearful disgrace. It seemed to me that the whole world must be looking at us with hatred and contempt, that the words "a *Potemkin* man" had become a synonym for treachery and cowardice. I seemed to hear around me the clamour of the public indignation, and I realised that I myself, as one who had taken part in the rising, shared the disgrace of that surrender.... I thought with horror of the trial, at which I should stand before the whole world, and, it seemed to me, face the curses of the people. From this feeling a dread of the trial grew upon me, and a passionate desire to escape from it, to free myself from the shame of being one of the *Potemkin* men!

I looked forward greedily to the newspaper, and when I had got it, I dreaded opening it. I expected columns of abuse of us in its pages.

Before the surrender I had borne my arrest with a brave heart. The days that had gone before had given me the strength to face the future with courage.... The surrender besmirched the glory of the past. For the time it vanished, and only one word, "betrayal," remained in its place.

So, I spent three weeks.

****

Ten days after our arrest we were transferred to the forwarding prison. On the morning of that day someone told Koshuba that we were to be taken that night to Sevastopol, and preparations were going on all day in the guard-house. A sort of clerk visited us and took down a detailed cross-examination of us as to our names, our rank, and so on. Several more companies of soldiers came into the yard. In the evening we began to hear the jingle of officers' spurs and words of command.

At two o'clock in the night the door of my cell was opened, and the sergeant on duty called out the customary "Get ready."

I hurriedly pulled on my boots, slipped on my soldier's great-coat, and, escorted by several soldiers, who were waiting for me at the door,

I went out to the room where all the soldiers not on duty usually sat. A smoky lamp dimly lighted up a moving mass of men. . . . . In the centre of the room stood all the sailors arrested in Theodosia, all dressed in soldiers' uniforms, and around them were standing soldiers with rifles. . . . Among them a sergeant was hurrying up and down giving some whispered explanations.

Through the dense veil of night, I could make out soldiers, too, in the street and the yard. . . . In the darkness everything took fantastic shape, and one might have fancied that these were brigands engaged in some dreadful deed. . . . But then an officer came in, called over the names, shouted a command, and we set off on our journey. Koshuba and I walked side by side; we were in good spirits.

"We shall be all the nearer our sailor lads; they won't let us come to hurt! And we shall see all the sooner what's going to happen," said Koshuba.

The other sailors were, on the other hand, very downcast. They had somehow got it into their heads that we were being taken away to execution. . . . And there certainly was something sinister in all this procession. . . . The tramp of two hundred men rang out strangely in the stillness of the night. Bayonets in front, bayonets each side, bayonets behind. . . . We came out into streets more and more deserted, and at last into the open country. . . . And by some strange circumstance, just as we came out into the open country, we heard somewhere a shot fired.

And the idea of execution would obtrude itself. One could not help thinking that in another month we should be led out like this, and every step would bring us nearer and nearer to that terrible end. . .

But at last a prison rose up before us. . . . Slowly the heavy gates parted, and a courtyard black as the pit swallowed us up. Again, a calling-over and a search, after which we were all put in the transferring prison. Here I first had a chance of talking with the other sailors, and learning their state of mind.

That depression of spirits, which one felt the last few days on the *Potemkin*, was apparent in these comrades too. The glorious days of the *Potemkin*'s power were forgotten; now, instead, came the thought of surrender, their comrades' betrayal, and ahead of them—the naked block. . . . And though the sailors did not give open expression to their fear, one felt in them some wound that had gone deep. It came out strikingly in their attitude towards any attempt at escape. That day there was a chance of escaping from the forwarding prison. We could all have run away, but the sailors protested earnestly, and did their utmost to dissuade Koshuba and me, who had made up our minds to attempt it. "They'll catch you just the same, and it will be all the worse for you; as it is, maybe they'll be merciful," they argued. Zadorozhny alone looked calmly, and with a shade of Little Russian humour, at the position.

Koshuba was entirely different. I met him twice a day at mealtimes, and was struck by his power of filling his life with interest. He was passing through his initiation into the movement.

"Such happiness I came in for today," Koshuba said to me one day. "You know, I had a visitor—a girl—a comrade, one of ourselves. She looked at me so mournfully—so mournfully—and blew a kiss to me."

And there was such rapture, such keen delight in his eyes when he uttered the words "a girl—a comrade," that I could not help being moved by it, and feeling that something good and blessed had happened to me, too, that day. . . .

Sometimes he would begin singing me verses he had made upon the glorious days on the Black Sea and the sailors' hard lot. It was his favourite pursuit.

Love for the "sailor lads" filled his whole heart, and showed itself in an extreme idealization of them. Before the mutiny he had loved them as a merry, gallant set of men; now he was filled with admiration of them as the first champions of the people. . . . All the more terrible for him was the cold-blooded cruelty of Tchuhnin in forcing those very "sailor lads" to shoot Koshuba.

****

We were only kept for twenty-four hours in the forwarding prison, but in that brief time there was a chance of escape. The common criminals, hearing that we were expecting to be executed, resolved to help us to escape, and made a simple and excellent plan for the purpose. The windows of the forwarding prison looked out into a small, empty courtyard which was used for exercise. There was no special sentinel in it, but from time to time sentinels on duty in other parts of the prison looked into it in passing. The following plan was formed: At six o'clock in the evening, when, as exercise was over, the yard was left empty, we were to break through the wall with a crowbar which was given us. As the walls were thin, this work should not have taken us more than a couple of hours.

Then through the hole broken in the wall, we were to get into the yard, and from there, with the help of a "cat"—a special contrivance made of a cord tied on to a sort of iron anchor, which is thrown up and hooks on to the wall—to climb over the wall into the street. There "our own people," who had been informed by the common criminals of the proposed escape, were to be waiting for us. The completely isolated and unguarded position of the forwarding department permitted us to carry on the work without any risk of being noticed, and the common criminals would have warned us of the sentinels coming by singing aloud.

But this plan failed through our own blundering. In the morning, before we knew anything about it, we asked the superintendent of the prison to let us have exercise. He refused. Then we insisted on seeing him, and declared we would smash up everything in the rooms, if our request were not granted. The old man promised to let us have exercise.

And at six o'clock in the evening, when it was time to begin work, we were summoned to exercise. By refusing to go after such insistence upon it, we should have roused suspicion at once. After our walk was over, the women had their exercise in the yard. . . . It was eight o'clock before we could begin work on the wall. And alas! half an hour later we were called away: the escort had come for us.

****

We are in the prison railway-van. Sentinels stand with bare sabres at the doors. The rest of the soldiers of the escort sit about between the prisoners, who are divided up, a couple on each seat.

An officer enters. . . . We hear the cruel and brutal words: "At the slightest attempt to escape, use your weapons. Kill without mercy."

"Yes, sir," answers the sergeant. The officer retires. . . . A bell rings . . . and the station platform is moving away from us.

Everything was at once changed in the compartment. The guards dropped their assumed severity, and were transformed into good-natured Russian soldiers. Tobacco and vodka appeared. . . . Songs were struck up. Tales and coarse anecdotes were to be heard on all sides. A sickly-looking little soldier, who was under arrest, was particularly communicative. He was being sent to the military hospital at Simferopol, to be examined as to his sanity. He had been an orderly. "I wasn't put into the ranks, and so here I am, more of a hen than a soldier." But in his comparatively short term of service he had already run away three times. He had been caught, put in prison, beaten; but nothing could cure him. He would stay on quietly for four months, and then again, he "was off." Now he was at last being sent to the hospital.

"But why do you run away from the service? Were you unhappy? Is it a hard life?" I asked him.

"Hard? No. The service is all right. I'd a good officer; he didn't beat me. And I was his wife's sweetheart, too. . . ."

Then followed a coarse expression, which set all the soldiers guffawing.

"Then why did you run away? You knew they would punish you for it," I went on.

"Well, something draws me on. I stay quiet for a while, and then it gets hold of my head. . . . Somehow I've a longing for the country. . . . Then I let all my service go, take a little money, and off I run!"

"But now, you know, if the doctors say you're all right, you'll be put in a disciplinary battalion."

"Well, what then? I shall run away from there. . . ." And turning away from me he began describing to the soldiers how he became the lover of his officer's wife. . . .

. . . Two o'clock at night. . . . Everything in the compartment hushed in sleep, except one bold voice talking of the *Tsar*, of oppression and revolution. It's Koshuba talking to his guards. . . . His eyes are glowing, he feels no fatigue as his inspired words flow on. . . .

And the train rushes on. . . .

The full moon lights up the meadows, covered with ricks of new-mown hay. The fragrance of the hay! How one longs to throw oneself in it! Is it possible that I shall never, never again sniff its intoxicating fragrance? . . .

The train rushes on. . . . "No, no, never again; no, no, never again," its wheels hum to me.

How one longs to break away to freedom! . . . If for one moment, for one hour only, to drink one's fill of life, to seize it all, in all its richness! Then one could die. . . . A moment; only one moment of freedom. . . . And how little men know how to value life, freedom! . . . How unconscious they are of it every minute, every hour! . . . Here we have dashed past a peasant. . . . And he goes his way quietly about the fields, unconscious of his freedom, of the happiness he possesses. And all men are like that. I did not feel it in earlier days. . . . But if once I were out there in freedom now, how precious life would be to me! . . .

"No, no, never again; no, no, never again," the wheels drone mockingly.

Monotonously the fields fly past, and it seems as though life itself were flying by as swiftly, as monotonously. . . and it will stop as quickly, as this train. Can it be that I must lay down life like that; that I can't break away from their clutches?

Everyone seems asleep...all is still....Warily I turn my head, scrutinise the sentinels...they are asleep....Leap out at once...a moment and I should be in freedom!..

But the doors are fastened with strong locks, and the windows are barred.... "No, no, never again...no, no, never again," the wheels chant in malicious triumph....

At ten o'clock we reached the station of Janko, and there we stayed for four hours, waiting for the train from Kharkoff. Our compartment, detached from the other carriages, did not wait in the station but was shunted into a siding some way off.

Through the barred windows we could see nothing but the roofs of the station buildings—not a soul, not a sign of life all round... except now and then a labourer passing in a blue jacket, or a heavy engine slowly rumbling through with an endless chain of goods-trucks after it....

Meanwhile life within the prison-van was in full swing. Our guards had fetched boiling water, and were slowly and with relish sipping their tea to the accompaniment of much coarse talk. The other inmates of the cage were munching bread and salt, and sausages as black as coal, and casting appealing glances at the soldiers in the hope of getting a mug of the yellow liquid from them.

I sat down by some of the soldiers and got into conversation with them. We talked of the service, of the movement among the people, and finally of the *Potemkin*. From this talk I saw that there was a spirit of revolt hidden here, too, and that these men felt sympathetic to the revolutionary movement, and were loyal to *Tsarism* from fear of the lash.

But in them a spirit of opposition was associated with extraordinary submissiveness and readiness to carry out orders. In spite of their perfectly friendly and sympathetic attitude to us, they kept a sharp look-out on us, and would not have thought twice about using their weapons and cruelly punishing us on the first attempt at escape. This fact was strikingly apparent in some incidents of their life in Siberia, told me by one of the soldiers with whom I talked. They were taking some political prisoners through Turkestan.

The escort were a good set—all soldiers who had been reached by the propaganda. The relations between the soldiers and the politicals were quite those of comrades. But one of the politicals formed a plan of escape, and when the soldiers were not looking, jumped out of window. He did this, however, so unsuccessfully, that he fell unconscious beside the sentry-box of a guard on the railway-line. The latter, seeing him, took him in. Half an hour later the soldiers ran up from the train, which had been stopped, and seeing the political, they maltreated him in a most cruel way. In their frenzy they even cut off the unfortunate man's fingers.

To my astonishment the soldier who told me this story commended their cruel action, and expressed the opinion that he would have done just the same.

"What, be like comrades, and all at once act like brutes?" I observed.

"But don't you think he was a brute? Wasn't he getting the guards into a disciplinary battalion? And they had wife and children at home. Get to your destination and then run away. You'll get no one into trouble then, anyway. Then I'd help you myself. And I'll tell you what happened to one political. The escort brought him to the place of destination, and within a month he ran off. He got to the railway-station and hadn't a farthing in his pocket. What was he to do? . . . He sits there grizzling over his luck, when someone slaps him on the back. He looks round, and there's one of his old escort party before him. Well, they got to talking in a friendly way, and what do you think? Those very escort soldiers collected him the money for his ticket among themselves. . . ."

"Yes, it was very well," I interrupted, "that he was sent to a free settlement. He knew he could run away from there. But with me it's like this: it's escaping on the road or on the gallows!"

The soldier hung his head in a shamefaced way; a sort of sick look passed over his face.

"Why the gallows? One can escape from prison," he said; but feeling at once the insincerity of his words, he added, with a sort of intense mournfulness: "*Ach*, brother, and I'd like to let you go. Doesn't it make me sick myself to take a man to execution? But I've not the strength. When I think of the government and a law-court—it's like facing a wild beast. Try and escape, and I should put an end to it. It's not myself but my hand would let fly the bullet. . . ."

The whistle of an engine was heard not far off, and the sound of a train approaching.

"Get ready!" commanded the sergeant, coming in.

Everything was transformed. . . .

The soldiers drew their sabres, and again assumed their stern and consequential bearing. We were formed in a double Indian file with two soldiers each side of each couple, and in that order, we moved to the prison-van of the Kharkoff train, where we were to be put in charge of a fresh set of guards.... In a few minutes we found ourselves in a long prison-van full of criminals of all classes.... Here were workmen, exiled by administrative order, soldiers, and even a few seamen. I was delighted to see new people, and joined a group consisting of several old peasant-workmen and a sailor.

There was a rather lively conversation going on between them. An old grey-haired workman was describing his wanderings. In his long life he had been all over Russia, on the Volga, and in the Ural, and the Caucasus, and the Crimea; and everywhere he had seen terrible poverty and suffering. All he had seen had stirred a spirit of protest in his heart, and, in spite of his advanced years, he was glowing with the divine fire of hatred for tyranny. His latter years he had spent in St. Petersburg, and he had taken part in Father Gapon's procession. Through information given by spies the police had banished him and his comrades to a provincial town.

But when they had been brought by *étape* to the place of their exile, the authorities there had refused to receive them, and had sent them on by *étape* to another town. But there the same story was repeated. And in this way, they had been for seven months travelling by *étape* from one town to another. Now they were being sent from Kharkoff to Simferopol. But they were going there without the faintest hope of being set free there. "Why don't you protest?" But how is one to protest? Do you suppose we are the only ones treated so? Nowadays there are so many in the same case. The other day we met a party of five men who had been tossing about for half a year.... And there's a special name they give us—*étapniks* they call us."

From further conversation, I learned that there exists a whole class of men who spend years of their lives being forwarded by *étape*. Among these travelling prisoners were also a great many common criminals, travelling from town to town at government expense, and everywhere being refused the hospitality of the prison. This class had greatly increased in numbers with the increased activity of the police in whole provinces of Russia.

While we were talking of this, the train arrived at Simferopol, and the sergeant of the escort called the *étapniks*, I was left alone with the sailor, who looked like an old marine. Our conversation turned on escapes from the prison at Sevastopol. The old sailor assured me that escape was only possible from the prisons on dry land. It was especially easy, he said, to escape from the marine barracks, where the guard consisted of sailors, all entirely devoted to the revolution. The one place from which escape was utterly impossible was a floating prison. "Once you're in there—it's a rat-trap. . . . You'll never get out," the sailor told me.

★★★★★★★★★★

Night was falling when we reached Sevastopol.

A guard, sent on purpose for us, surrounded us at the station, and led us to the marine barracks. Not without a thrill did I enter the town to which our eyes had been constantly turned all through the mutiny. Here were the squadron and the most progressive men of the fleet, on whose word the success of the rising depended. . . . Eagerly we listened for every sound coming from it. . . . But Sevastopol maintained an enigmatic silence.

And when everything was over, and the *Potemkin* had surrendered, we still went on hoping that Sevastopol would speak—would speak so that its voice would shake the throne to its foundations. . . . At the bottom of our hearts there lurked a hope even that our comrades the sailors would rescue us. . . .

I strained my eyes, peering into the dark streets, fancying every moment that a detachment of marines would come to meet us. . . . The news that we were being taken to the barracks gave me courage, and hopes, one brighter than another, floated before my imagination. In the barracks we were put into two large cells.

As soon as the soldiers escorting us had retired, the sailors ran up to our doors with faces of welcome. . . . Some of the *Potemkin* men met their old comrades here. Greetings, questions were showered upon us. But the news the sailors told us was bad. The whole fleet had been disarmed; the shells had been unloaded from the battleships; all the rifles had been taken away from the barracks; armed infantry soldiers had been put into many of the ships. Arrests were going on in all the branches of the services; more than three thousand sailors had been arrested; all the prisons, the fortresses, the town lock-up stations, and the floating prisons were overflowing, and the *Pruth*, had just lately been transformed into a prison-ship! (A torpedo transport, which mutinied at the same time as the *Potemkin*; but, in spite of its efforts, did not succeed in joining us, and was taken by torpedo-boats.)

★★★★★★★★★★

There were rumours that thirty-five sailors had been shot without trial, that the others would receive severe punishment.... Some were, however, more optimistic in their tone, and said the *Tsar* himself was taking the matter up, that Tchuhnin was being forced to resign, and that the sailors who were found guilty would get off easily.

I did not, naturally, attach any significance to the latter story, but considered the former rumours more probable. Crushed by this bad news, I did not sleep all night.... At eight o'clock we were ordered to get ready, and led out into the courtyard.

There stood a platoon of sailors and a marine officer. They were only waiting for rifles for the sailors escorting us, and men had been sent to fetch them from the soldiers' barracks. (There were not twenty rifles left in all the barracks of the Russian Fleet, so thorough were the measures taken to secure the victory of the *Tsarism* over the mutiny.)

At last the rifles were brought, and we set off. The sailors guarding us told us that they were taking us to the floating prison—the *Pruth*, And soon we were led to the shore and put into a sloop. There could be no more doubt; we were being taken to the floating prison! "*When you're once in there—it's a rat-trap! You'll never get out!*" ... I thought of the old sailor's words.

It was a magnificent June morning. The sun was shining gaily, plunging her burning rays in the cool waves, which seemed swooning languorously under her hot caresses.... Everything spoke of life, of beauty, and oh! the longing for life ... while we were getting nearer to the tomb.... I wanted to shout: "I want to live!" to shout so that the whole world might hear me!

But I was afraid of the smile of triumph on the face of our butchers, and I was dumb.... I longed to speak glowing words of brotherhood, of love, of the beauty of life.... But the butchers were all round me; I dreaded meeting with jeers and mockery ... and I was silent. I longed to throw myself into the waves to soothe my tortured nerves in their cold embraces. But the butchers were sitting at the sides of the boat, ready to run me through at the slightest movement.

And we were getting nearer and nearer to the tomb. At last the sloop drew alongside the ladder of the *Pruth*. The sailor on duty ran to report to the captain. But the latter came to the top of the ladder, and declared that he could not take us aboard, as there were no more cells free in the ship.

A moment of agonising suspense, of vague hopes ... and suddenly a voice is heard, shattering these hopes:

"There are the dark cells."

We were taken on deck, where we were met by the captain, surrounded by marine officers, and with them an army officer of some sort. The latter, who performed conscientiously and zealously the duties of a gaoler on board the ship, summoned some soldiers, who searched us and led us away to the prison part of the ship—*i.e.*, to the hold. The small opening leading to the hold was almost completely darkened by hangings of tarpaulin, so that too much air and light might not penetrate to the prisoners. We found ourselves in a fearful stench and darkness as soon as we got into it.

The air was only changed by means of one ventilator and tiny port-holes, such as are commonly seen in the holds of big steamers. In hastily constructed cells, calculated to hold some eight men at most, with two or three such port-holes, twenty or thirty sailors were confined. It was so hot and stifling that the sailors were sitting completely undressed. The place was so crowded that at the slightest movement the men trampled, on one another, and the soldiers standing on guard were soaking with sweat. . . . And with all this myriads of bugs. . . .

In the light solitary cells it was somewhat better. . . .

We were put into separate cells. . . . I found myself in absolute darkness and a stifling atmosphere. I felt as though I were underground. . There was not a breath of fresh air, and the scalding side of the ship, which adjoined my cell, made it fearfully hot. (Later on I learned from the investigating magistrate in charge of my case that the wall of my cell was specially heated by the engines close by it.) I was without light and air. . . . And the exquisite sea was splashing against the wall of the cell. . . . And the stream of life was flowing overhead. Men were running merrily to and fro, singing merry songs. . . . And again came the longing for life, the longing for freedom and space once more. . . . But I was in a tomb and gaolers all round me. I longed to break open the door, to rush out into the air, and then to die. . . .

But an iron padlock hung on the door. . . . Then I fell to weeping and sobbing, but soon this feeling of misery and anguish changed to wild hatred and thirst for vengeance. . . .

My cell was about seven feet square, and when I stood upright, my head touched the ceiling. It was not a cell, but a cage. Feeling about, I found a hammock and flung myself down in it. The three preceding nights without sleep had their effect now; I slept the sleep of the just.

Waking up, I felt my body burning, and something big and crawling creeping over me. I threw off my shirt in horror, and passed my hand over my bare body, and in a second felt that hundreds of bugs were crawling over my arm. I was covered all over with swarms of bugs! I began knocking at my door, but received the answer that the petty officer had gone away with the keys. I tried to brush the filthy creatures off, but they kept swarming over me in fresh legions. At last I succeeded in getting rid of them. My body was covered with bites. A fearful irritation set up, and I was soon bleeding and sore. I made up my mind not to touch the hammock again, and spent the whole time I was on the *Pruth* in walking up and down.... I got some sleep standing up....

I had hardly disposed of the bugs, before I discovered some other inhabitants of my cage. I suddenly heard a squeak, and something ran between my legs. I began feeling about, not knowing what to think, but soon it was explained—these were rats. They came out in extraordinary numbers, ran scurrying to and fro about my feet, and got into my boots. I drove them away, but they came again in crowds. ... I had obviously been cast into this place to force me to beg for mercy; but I was stubbornly silent.... In this way the autocracy was celebrating its victory.

★★★★★★★★★★

Sailors of very different parts of the Fleet were imprisoned on the *Pruth*, The awful conditions of their imprisonment and the stories they had to tell of punishment inflicted and to come could not but have a most depressing effect on the minds of the prisoners, who belonged almost exclusively to the less intelligent and less advanced sections of the navy. They were all in the clutches of panic. A sort of crushed hopelessness had settled upon them all.... And at times terrible whispers of treachery were heard among them.... The quartermaster—one of the *Potemkin* crew who had returned from Roumania—distinguished himself in this respect.

One day a colonel of *gendarmerie* came aboard to gather evidence. I was summoned to him. After a brief examination, he ordered somebody to be brought. The soldiers led in the quartermaster.

"Is this he?" asked the *gendarme*, pointing to me.

"Yes, your honour."

"What was he called on the *Potemkin*?"

"Ivanov Matveiev, your honour!"

Then followed details of my "criminal activity." In an hour's time I was led back to my cell. I was absorbed in meditating over all that had passed, when the clink of spurs on the stairs leading to our part of the ship made me all attention.

"Unlock the cell," said a voice, which I recognised as the same *gendarme* colonel's.

They opened a cell close by.

"Your name's Ivan Zadorozhny?" I heard through the wall.

"Yes, your honour."

"Do you know him?" continued the colonel, apparently addressing the quartermaster, who had turned informer.

"Yes, your honour. He took the leading part, was one of the committee, killed the officers...."

The latter assertion was an obvious falsehood, as Zadorozhny was one of the engineers, and during the time of the mutiny was in his battery, where he even concealed one of the officers.

"If you know me, say in what capacity I served," Zadorozhny answered, promptly.

"In the machinery department," answered the quartermaster.

The informer was caught in the lie. The rest of his evidence was in the same spirit.

The news of this betrayal had a crushing effect on the prisoners. A spirit of mutual distrust crept in among them. Every hour there were rumours of fresh treachery.

The one man who could dispel the cloud hanging over us was Koshuba. The little man so unattractive in appearance would come out of his cell to dinner.

"Ay, lads, why be downhearted?" we would hear his cheerful voice, and at once everything brightened up, as though a ray of sunshine had broken through a black pall of storm-clouds.

Songs were struck up, laughter was heard, and in a few minutes one would not have recognised us as the same careworn people....

On the third day of my stay on the *Pruth*, I was summoned to the captain's cabin. As soon as I entered, I saw Alexeieff there. At that time, I had not formed a clear judgment of his actions on the *Potemkin*, and the sight of a man with whom I had gone through such experiences made me forget my old antipathy for him. I rushed up with unfeigned pleasure and held out my hand to him. But he turned coldly away and, not responding to my greeting, said:

"Yes, this is he."

Only then I observed the same *gendarme* colonel was also present. I had obviously been summoned here for identification.

Before I had time to recover from the shock, the soldiers were leading me out. I was shaking all over with indignation, and a cry of "Scoundrel!" broke involuntarily from my lips, when I had passed out of the cabin door.

I don't know whether Alexeieff heard it, but I don't suppose it reached the conscience of the "honest *bourgeois*." Next day my name was discovered, and the day after I was transferred to a civil prison.

On the morning of that day the captain of the *Pruth* informed me that I was to be moved, and at four o'clock the petty officer on duty told me to get ready.

The bitter moment of parting from my comrades and from Koshuba had come. The latter, seeing me led out, knocked frantically at the door of his cell. I rushed to him, the soldiers tried to detain me, but with a violent effort, I tore myself out of their grasp, and ran to Koshuba

****

The cutter steamed swiftly and noisily to the shore. But now I could not be glad of what I had so passionately desired before. The thought of Koshuba left alone fretted me incessantly. His face at the moment of farewell was continually before me, and in his eyes, I read a dumb reproach for deserting him. And his last flaming words of vengeance kept ringing in my ears. . . .

Meanwhile the cutter reached the shore, and a rough shove from one of the soldiers roused me from my reverie.

Half an hour later I found myself in the large well-lighted ward of a prison hospital.

On the morning of the next day the investigating magistrate, a marine court-martial judge, Colonel Voevodsky, made his first interrogation of me in the presence of the military prosecutor for marine cases.

On the ground of the district being under martial law, I was to be tried before a martial marine court, on the charge (under Article 100) of an armed attempt upon the integrity of the Imperial Power in Russia. The accusation was based principally on that one of my speeches, in which I urged the sailors to fire on the town. Detailed evidence in regard to it was given by Midshipman Kalyuzhny, who happened to be present at it.

In conversation with me, the investigating magistrate tried to get support for the idea that the mutiny on the island Tendro had not arisen spontaneously from the provocation given by the officers, but was the outcome of a preconcerted plan on the part of the leaders among the sailors. He assumed that they had arranged with the steward of the mess, who served the meat, to provide maggoty meat so as to rouse the crew. In their wisdom the judges had positively come to the point of suspecting that I knew of the mutiny before the arrival of the *Potemkin* at Odessa, and had promised the sailors my assistance beforehand. In fact, it was the usual story of the investigating ingenuity of Russian judges, trying to convert every spontaneous mass movement into the planned and concerted work of revolutionary societies.

Without wasting time in disproving these charges, I declared myself a Social Democrat, and asserted that I went aboard the *Potemkin* to fight for a Constituent Assembly on the basis of the fourfold formula (*i.e.*, elected by direct, secret, universal, and equal suffrage).

"And what is the punishment awaiting me by Article 100?" I asked Voevodsky among other things.

The colonel hesitated.

"You needn't mind, I am ready for anything."

"The death penalty at the worst; penal servitude at the best."

"And will the trial be soon?" I went on.

"Oh, not for some time yet. I don't expect it will take place for three or four months at least. You see, there are seven hundred prisoners in your case!"

"But they are in Roumania!" I observed in surprise.

"Well, what of that?" answered the colonel, with the coolness of a Jesuit. "Today they're in Roumania, tomorrow they'll be in Russia...."

Obviously, he was hinting at the possible extradition of the *Potemkin* men by the Roumanians.

Promising to let me have an interview with my relatives when the material for my case had been finally collected, the colonel retired.

The hospital building of the Sevastopol prison was in a special small court, one wall of which adjoined the female prison, while the other gave on to the street. The complete absence of sentinels, with the exception of one superintendent on duty in the hospital, of itself turned one's thoughts to plans of escape. Before getting into relations with my comrades, I made up my mind to make a closer acquaintance with the superintendents in charge of me. There were—as is the custom in all posts in Russian prisons—two of these, relieving each other every six hours. One of them turned out to be a Pole.

From conversation I learned that his views inclined to the Opposition, that he was only serving in the prison because he knew no trade; that he was sick of the prison service, and would be glad to throw it up. He had left Poland simply because he was ashamed for his comrades to see him a prison official. He told me a great deal about his own country, and the bloody fusillades he had witnessed, and he spoke of all this so sincerely that I could feel no doubt of the man's honesty. All this so disposed me in his favour that after three days' acquaintance I proposed that he should run away one night with me. The Pole listened with great attention to my plan, considered escape quite possible, but promised to give me a final reply in the evening. Two hours afterwards he was off duty. His next shift would only begin at twelve o'clock at night.

The time dragged on wearisomely, and at last it struck midnight. I heard a noise in the corridor; the superintendent was relieved. But to my surprise the Pole did not come to me. I spent several hours more in agonies of suspense, and at last, making up my mind that he was still undecided, I lay down to sleep.

Next morning, however, I began to have suspicions of the Pole's sincerity. Chance favoured me. My prison comrades had handed a newspaper to me, and, knowing that the Pole was on duty immediately, I began reading it without taking any precautions.

All at once someone ran out of the yard to my window, and calling, "Hide the paper; your superintendent has seen it and reported to the authorities," disappeared before I had time to see who it was. Though I did not quite believe this information, I did conceal the paper. A few minutes later the senior superintendent actually did come into my cell and demand the paper.

"You can look, if you like," I answered.

The search was without result, as I had hidden the paper in a very unlikely place.

"What did you call me for?" the senior official grumbled to the Pole.

"Why, I saw the paper in his hands myself," the latter replied, penitently.

"You're a clever one at watching them," muttered his superior; and he walked out of the cell.

"What did you betray me for?" I asked the Pole.

"Well, you shouldn't read so that all the exercise party can see you. I can't get the sack on your account."

But this reply did not satisfy me, and I suspected the Pole of treachery. My suspicions were not without foundation. The same day, I was transferred from the hospital to the prison itself, and a week later I learned through comrades that the Pole had reported all our conversation to the prison authorities.

Being transferred to the prison building was not, however, much cause of regret to me, though the hope of immediate escape vanished, and the supervision was much stricter. I was delighted to find myself among comrades, who gave me a very warm welcome. Getting into close touch with them and telling them all about the *Potemkin* set me thinking over the whole story of it again; and, as by this time the first period of acute sorrow over the surrender of the *Potemkin* had passed, I could look at it calmly and objectively.

I no longer looked on the *Potemkin* mutiny as an "adventure," as I had described it in a letter to my friends from the prison hospital. Now I saw it as one of the great landmarks of the revolution. The sense that I had had a hand in it inspired me with a new impulse of courage.... The trial was no longer a terror to me, and once more I held my head high when I thought of it.

A week later I received the first note from my friends outside, who had arrived in Sevastopol to attempt a rescue. These were its contents:

Key;
Town where N. used to live
Town where M. was arrested
Town where G. lived in exile
Town where K. lived in the year 19—
Town where you were living in the year 19—
With aid of this key work out a fuller one.

******

By the "key" is meant the words by means of which the notes are deciphered. Usually the pages of some book are used, but in this case the names of these towns served the purpose.

******

Then followed some lines in cipher, in which my comrades inquired whether I had any hope of escape and what was necessary for that end. The correspondence was very cleverly arranged. It made use of such a key that our "postman" could not find it out. At the same time the key was itself a proof of its genuine origin, as only intimate friends could know such details of the life of my comrades.

I immediately composed a reply, in which I arranged the method of using the cipher, begged them to tell me who had come, and suggested the possible means of escape. The correspondence was organised, and we passed to the consideration of escape, for the organisation of which several active and experienced comrades had been sent, belonging to the following societies: the Odessa Committee of the Social Democratic party, the Odessa Committee of the Bund, the Kiev Committee of the group of the Minority. The Sevastopol Committee also took part in it.

Inside the prison another "amalgamated" committee of a sort was formed, consisting of a Social Democrat I will call N., a Social Revolutionist, and me. Later on, another Social Revolutionist called Myshkin also joined it. Every step, every plan, was considered by us all. That I might not be detected in the correspondence, our "postman" brought the notes from the free world outside to one of the members of our little committee, usually to N., who deciphered them, drew his own conclusions, and sent them on to me. I thought them over, and if there were any serious question in them, passed them on to the other comrades. Then, drawing my conclusion from all their opinions, I sent an answer to the comrades in freedom in the same order—*i.e.*, passed it first to N., who put it into cipher and gave it to the "postman." We decided first of all to send our free comrades a plan of the prison.

For two days we worked at it, and, at last, after unanimously agreeing as its to accuracy, we sent it to our free comrades. In a week, out of a mass of suggestions and plans, two projects stood out. The first, suggested by us, was attended with greater risk; there were many chances of being caught in the hue and cry that would be raised within three or four minutes of my escape. The second plan, which was that of our comrades outside, was attended with less risk, might reckon, in fact, on almost certain success. But at least a fortnight would be needed to elaborate it. And the latter circumstance made the second plan seem out of the question to the prison committee.

The point was that I was to be tried by court-martial, and was imprisoned in a town which was under martial law. Owing to the information given by the hospital superintendent, the authorities had been warned of my project of escape. Their suspicions were getting keener every day, and the guard over me was more and more strictly kept as the days went on.

All this gave grounds for supposing that I might be transferred to one of the prison-ships. And so, delay was the greatest risk of all. It might well lead to an absolute impossibility of escape.

Moreover, with bold and determined men, the first scheme had a good chance of success. And therefore, the prison committee urged the adoption of our plan. We had, however, to give way to the free comrades, as it appeared that a great number of comrades would be exposed to danger by our scheme. The "free men" set to work to pave the way for their scheme, and I had to wait in patience. . . .

For several days everything went on smoothly. The free comrades let me hear every day of the progress of their preliminary measures. I kept exceedingly quiet, avoided any cause of offence to the prison officials, and even fancied that I had succeeded in disarming their suspicions.

But one day I irritated the governor of the prison.

My cell was on the fourth storey. I had an excellent view of all that went on in the street, and so I earnestly begged one of my free comrades to walk by the prison. My comrade consented to do so, and one day he walked several times to and fro before the prison.

This interview threw me into such an ecstasy that I began shouting a revolutionary song at the top of my voice. The governor of the prison at once walked across the courtyard.

"Shut up! leave off singing!" my comrades called to me; but, delirious with delight, I did not heed them, but went on recklessly. I came to my senses when I found myself in another cell on the first storey, where the enraged governor had ordered the "nightingale" to be removed.

"Welcome, comrade!" I heard a soft and pleasant voice, as soon as the superintendent had slammed the door of my new abode.

I looked round and saw whence it came. My next neighbour evidently shared the opening in the wall, and was speaking through it. Standing on a bench I could talk to the comrade, though I could not see him. He told me he was a Social Revolutionist, and his name was Myshkin. My meeting with him was such a bright spot in my prison life, that I cannot forbear sharing my recollections of him with the reader.

As I gained a more intimate acquaintance with the revolutionary world, I had reflected mournfully that one must not confound the champions of ideas with the ideas themselves. The type of idealistic revolutionist, who lives single-heartedly in his ideas and carries the element of idealism into every action of his life, is more and more rarely to be met with in the revolutionary world. And of late, since the revolution has gained ground among vast masses of the population, such idealistic types have become exceptions among intellectual revolutionists. But Myshkin revived before me the type of the revolutionist of the seventies.

At the time when I met him, he had been over three years in solitary confinement, awaiting trial. His comrades, arrested upon the same case, had long ago been sent to Siberia, and some had by now served out their time and returned.

But simply through his acquaintance with Foma Katchura, Myshkin was suspected by the *gendarmes* of belonging to a "fighting organisation," and for the last three years the police had been looking for evidence against him. His comrades had forgotten him, and it was a year and a half since Myshkin had had an interview. But he did not blame his friends, nor had he lost faith in friendship; on the contrary, he put the ties of comradeship higher than anything. He explained the conduct of his comrades by the absence of sentimentality in them, and by their being engrossed by the cause.

"Revolutionists cannot live in personal life; they are called to the work, and must give up all their time and strength to it," he said to me. "I believe, really, that we ought to renounce personal life altogether. Think how much energy it absorbs." There was the fervour of the martyr in all his thoughts and motives.

The idea that there was beside him a comrade menaced by the death penalty weighed on Myshkin and tormented him. He showed the exquisite delicacy and sweetness of his character in his attitude to me and his efforts to support and cheer me. I felt every moment that there was a near and loving friend at my side, ready without hesitation to take my lot on himself.

But deep as was his sympathy for his comrades, and intense as was his love for them, he asked of them a proud and unflinching attitude to the enemy before all else.

"Not one prayer, not one sound of suffering, should they hear from our lips," he used often to say to me; "and if you want to preserve your spiritual balance, behave so that the enemy is impressed by your manliness. Remember that for the revolutionist the dearest thing in the world is honour, and if there is a spot on it, it poisons the last consolation—the sense of one's own rectitude; then your comrades will turn away from you, and I would be the first to throw mud at you!"

When he spoke like that, I felt that there would be no forgiveness in that gentle heart for such wrongdoing. During the hours I spent with Myshkin I forgot the prison and the death awaiting me. Before my mind floated the ideal of Socialism, in all its light and radiance, and the road to it, paved with agonies and strewn with corpses, along which the revolutionist proudly and gallantly marches forward, as resplendent as the idea that consecrates him. And when I thought of Myshkin, I thought that he would be one of those dead whose bodies lined that road. . . .

And I was not mistaken. . . . A month after his release from prison Myshkin was killed during the *pogrom* in Theodosia.

****

To carry out successfully the plan we had made, it was essential that I should be in another cell. By the advice of my comrades, I made up my mind to beg the governor of the prison, two days before I meant to escape, to move me into another cell on the ground that the cobbler working close to me prevented me from sleeping. As there was no cell free except the one needed for the success of our plans, we took for granted I should be transferred into that one.

When the governor came at six o'clock in the evening for the usual inspection, I accordingly appealed to him.

"But you have not to be here long, anyway. You are soon to be transferred to another prison!" was the reply I received—far worse than a refusal.

"Soon," in his mouth, meant "tomorrow."

Next day, then, I was to be removed to a ship or a prison from which escape would be impossible. . . .

On Myshkin this news had such a crushing effect that I positively had to try and console him. When we had at last somewhat recovered from the first shock of this sudden news, we both felt the impulse to struggle against the inevitable to the last moment. Again, we began going over in our minds every exit and entrance of the prison, and suddenly devised a new chance of escape. Everything might be arranged for the following night.

I put down all my plans on a sheet of paper and sent it to the other members of our committee. But by now it was four o'clock in the morning; our comrades were asleep, and could not get the note till the morning inspection.

In the morning I met N. at exercise. The news of my removal had affected him just as it had done Myshkin. He had already sent my note to the town, but, as though foreseeing it would be all in vain, he looked mournfully at me. On his way, after exercise, to his cell, he ran to the door of my cell, slid open the peep-hole in the door, and warmly squeezed my hand through it.

My comrade's emotion gained upon me, and I longed to see Myshkin. In spite of our great friendliness we had not seen each other.

The little opening through which we talked did not allow us to see each other's faces. We were both taken out to exercise at the same time, but we walked in different yards.

I spoke of my desire to Myshkin.

"Very well," he answered. "I will refuse my exercise today, and will sit at the window so that we shall see each other when you are led out to walk."

I looked forward impatiently to the hour of exercise.... And when the door of my cell was opened and the superintendent cried: "Come to exercise," I almost ran into the yard.

At the grating of Myshkin's window I saw two black eyes.... I saw nothing else ... nothing but those eyes full of melancholy and kindness.... I can never forget them!

Seeing me, Myshkin tried to smile encouragingly ... but at that moment the prison gates opened and two convoy soldiers came into the yard.

"For you!" Myshkin cried involuntarily.

He was right. A few minutes later I was told to get ready. When I approached the door of my cell, Myshkin began rapping furiously at his door. The superintendent, frightened, went quickly to open it, and we rushed up to each other....

"Farewell, and be brave," he whispered.

"Think of me," I answered.

In a few minutes I was walking across the prison yard to the gates. All my comrades were standing at their windows.

"Farewell, comrades!" I shouted to them.

"Till we meet, comrade!"

"We shall come for you yet!"

"We shall rescue you! ..." I heard voices from the prison.

The gate slammed.

****

We passed through hot and dusty streets. The heavy military greatcoat hanging on my shoulder stifled me, but I was even more oppressed by uncertainty. From talk with the soldiers I learned that I was being taken to the staff of the fortress, and from there was to be transferred to another prison. Of the latter the soldiers themselves knew nothing.

It was a public holiday, and in front of the hall of the staff there was a parade being held, at which Tchuhnin was to be present. The officers of the staff were taking part in the parade, and had to wait a long while for it to be over. I chanced to look into the street. The companies of soldiers and sailors standing picturesquely about in easy attitudes waiting for the parade, the groups of laughing officers, the jingle of the weapons, and the bright colours in the cheerful sunshine, made such a festive picture that I could not help admiring it.

For a moment I forgot that all these men had come here at the word of command, that at the word of command they would begin doing something utterly useless and of no interest to them. I fancied that they were all drawn together here by some one idea, some common interest or pleasure!

But then I heard a shout that was caught up and repeated along the ranks: "Attention!" The officers rushed to their places. The soldiers drew themselves up, and everything was rigid.... The soldiers' greeting sounded, came nearer, and died away at the windows of the building. Tchuhnin appeared before us.

A stout man of middle height, with a big head on a short neck, he gave the impression of a sort of octopus. And this octopus turned facing the sailors and began making a speech.

I looked round and saw my escort were entirely absorbed in the parade, and the door to the street was open.... Cautiously I took a few steps ... a moment ... and I should be free! Suddenly I heard the clink of spurs, and an officer stood facing me right in the doorway. The soldiers, too, heard the clink ... and the brief vision of freedom vanished again.....

"By order of the Commander-in-Chief, Vice-Admiral Tchuhnin, you will be transferred to the military guard-house," said the newcomer, addressing me. He was, I afterwards learned. Captain Olengrün, adjutant to the chief officer of the staff.

"Any statement in regard to books or goods or your other needs you can make to me personally when on my rounds. But I advise you to behave carefully. You know in the guard-house we have everything on a war footing. The rifles are loaded, and the guard is authorised to use weapons...."

"Soldiers!" he added, "lead the prisoner to the chief military guard-house."

The escort again surrounded me. The sun had already passed noon when we at last entered the guard-house. It was a monotonous-looking building, shut in on all sides by a high wall. A small door, beside which a sentinel continually paced up and down, led to a large, light room, filled with soldiers, who searched me, and led me through a long corridor to a cell. The heavy iron-covered door slammed behind me, and I found myself alone in a rather large and light room. At my first hurried look round, I perceived that escape from it was impossible. The thick walls, the high windows barred by solid gratings, the sentinels patrolling every door and window, the numbers of soldiers scattered about everywhere, made the idea of escape absurd and impracticable, and I was seized with wild fury against Tchuhnin, to whom I owed it that I was here.

. . . Pacing from corner to corner in this mood, I felt, with that special sense developed by solitary confinement, that someone was standing at the peep-hole in my door. I went up to the door.

"Don't you want to send anything to the town. Mr. Student?" I heard a voice through the peephole.

"And who are you?" I asked the speaker.

"A porter in the guard-house."

I naturally accepted his suggestion, and in a few minutes B. (so I will call my "postman") had set off to the town with a note. In the evening B. came into my cell and brought me a note from my comrades. Only then I had a good view of the man, who afterwards played such an important part in my life. From his long chestnut moustache, his rather Kalmuck head, his brown eyes, the endless humour and slyness twinkling in his face, he could be recognised at once as a Little Russian, and a clever, tricky, careless, merry fellow.

But one had to keep a sharp look-out on him, I felt. He would turn one round his finger.

"If you like, I can take another note tomorrow," he said.

"Very well," I answered; "we'll talk of it tomorrow."

B. seemed to meditate.

A few days passed in the emptiest correspondence, but it was evident that both parties—*i.e.,* myself and my free comrades on the one side and B. on the other—regarded this meaningless correspondence as something necessary, which must be followed by something else of real importance, and we and B. both felt that this was simply tuning our instruments, and the real performance was to come. But neither party could quite venture to begin on it.

In this state of expectancy, a week passed. Meanwhile the correspondence did not take up much of my time, and I had plenty to spare for observing the life of a military prison.

Externally it differed very little from that of the civil prison. At six o'clock in the morning the attendants, who were soldiers, came into the prisoners' cells and put out the lamps. A few minutes later the sergeant on duty opened the cells, the prisoners began making their *toilettes* and went to wash. The length of time spent in this *toilette* depended entirely on the sergeant.

If he were "a man," he opened all the cells at the same time, and the washing and dressing lasted for two or three hours, during which time the prisoners walked about the cells, talking together, and enjoying a respite from their solitary confinement, which was the more irksome in the military prison, as they were forbidden books and occupations of all sorts. It may well be imagined, that in such conditions, the interval for the morning *toilette* afforded a relief in the monotony of the prisoners' life, and they were deeply grateful to those sergeants who prolonged it. Their appreciation of a humane attitude to them was shown in a striking manner by an incident which took place in the Sevastopol guard-house shortly before I was there.

In a cell occupied by seven or eight men, the prisoners removed some boards from their wooden ceiling, hung a towel over the place, and were intending to escape by night through the opening thus prepared. But on the day fixed a sergeant who had treated the prisoners particularly well, went on duty, and so, when everything was ready, one of the prisoners said:

"I say, lads, you know we shall get the sergeant into trouble, and he's 'a man'; that's not right. We ought to put it on to another—some scoundrelly fellow."

The others agreed, and their escape was put off. But next day, unluckily, the good sergeant was on duty again, and again the prisoners put off decamping. This went on for five days, and all that time those men lived in a cell with an aperture in their ceiling, which could not be well concealed, and with the risk of its being discovered any minute, simply to avoid getting a sergeant who had treated them decently into trouble.

On the sixth day the opening was discovered.

On the other hand, when a sergeant regarded the prisoners as wild beasts he had to keep in their cage, they avenged themselves by every means at their disposal.

At ten o'clock in the morning the beating of a drum announced a new relief of soldiers, and all the cells were closed.

The inspection began. . . . Usually it took place in the presence of the two officers who were on duty that day in the guard-house. One of them, the captain of the watch, usually an officer of the rank of a lieutenant, was in charge of the guard-house in particular, the other, always a captain, was responsible for the day for the guard of the whole fortress of Sevastopol, but was generally to be found in the guard-house.

With few exceptions these officers were but little better than hooligans and members of the "Black Hundreds."

The prisoners, especially the politicals (there were at this time four soldiers imprisoned in the guardhouse for propaganda in the army), they treated with brutal hatred. One, for instance, happening to see some bowls for food in the cells of the prisoners at dinner-time, went so far as to shout that these "cattle" (the captain's expression) might eat out of their slop-pails.

They usually began by speaking very rudely to me, and only changed their tone after meeting with firm resistance. They seemed to hate me the more for those privileges I enjoyed in the guard-house—exercise, food at my own cost, and books. The latter especially roused the indignation of the officers. When they saw a heap of books on my table, they usually turned triumphantly to me.

"Ah! ... Books? ... Forbidden things? ... By what authorisation?"

"Look, if you like," I answered.

The gentlemen fell on the books, but alas! on all of them they found stamped:

"Passed by the Colonel of the Staff."

They flung the books on the floor in impotent spite, and tried other methods of annoyance.

"Why is that linen piled up under the bed?"

"Because I am allowed by the colonel of the staff to have my own linen."

"But it's not the place for it under the bed."

"Well, in that case, put a cupboard in the cell. . . ."

"Search him!" the captain would shout at last. The soldiers would begin to search me, and the captain would walk out of the cell with an air of well-bred indignation.

Very different was the behaviour of the staff officers, who had the direct and permanent control of the guard-house. There were three of them: Colonel Shemiakin, the chief officer of the fortress staff. Captain Olengrün, and another captain whose name I don't remember; and they all impressed me by their intelligence and the care they bestowed on the prisoners, and on me in particular.

On their weekly visit to the guard-house they always inquired about my needs, begged me to inform them in case of any brutal behaviour on the part of the officers, and promised to take steps to prevent it. My "postman" B., reported to me that they had even left special orders to the officers on duty to treat me with civility.

Inspection generally lasted till dinner-time. If there were a good sergeant on duty, the cells were opened again, and the prisoners spent a couple of hours together.

At six o'clock supper followed and evening inspection. Lamps were brought in, and the prisoners were locked up for the night.

But if the guard-house differed little in external order from the civil prison, the relations of the inhabitants were a striking contrast in the two institutions.

All the inhabitants of the civil prisons were sharply divided into two hostile camps: prisoners and gaolers.

It was quite different in the guard-house. The contrast between the external splendour and the inner weakness of the autocracy was very evident there. Only the most trifling percentage of the soldiers imprisoned in the guard-house were there on account of offences against the common law; the immense majority were in prison for military misdemeanours, desertion, failure to salute an officer, attack on a sergeant, etc. The punishments inflicted by the military courts for these offences were truly Draconian. In the cell opposite mine there was, for instance, a soldier of the reserves, condemned to twelve years' penal servitude. His crime was simply that when drunk he had declined to salute an officer.

When the latter ordered the police officer to arrest him, the soldier fell on his knees, and begging forgiveness, ventured to touch the officer's "most high honourable" hand. Such "insolence" infuriated the noble gentleman, and he presented the case in such a light that it appeared as though the soldier had attempted to strike him. The court-martial condemned him for this to penal servitude.

But this is not an exceptional instance of cruelty; it is a typical case of court-martial justice.

It is only natural that such prisoners should not feel themselves to be criminals. They consider themselves innocent men suffering from the despotism and injustice of the officers.

On the other hand, the soldiers who looked after the prisoners in the military guard-house did not regard themselves as gaolers. Having to serve once a month in the guard-house, they met there soldiers, like themselves, suffering for offences of which anyone of themselves might be accused at any moment, and the sentinels felt that the imprisoned soldiers were not enemies, but their own people. There was not the slightest feeling of hostility between them, and both sides understood perfectly well that they were placed in their apparently antagonistic position not of their own accord, not from any fault of theirs, but simply by the action of the hated officers.

And if the prisoners had made a mutiny, not one hand would have been raised against them. To quell such a rising the officers would have had to introduce the most depraved "units."

The reader perceives that the terrible words "the rifles are loaded, and the guards are authorised to use them," uttered by Captain Olengrün, were an empty phrase.

****

One day B. winked slyly as he handed me a letter from outside, and said:

"Well, now, Mr. Student, what about escaping?"

"Why, it wouldn't be amiss!" I answered calmly. "But can one get away from here?"

"You could get away if there were only the money."

"Very well," I said. "You talk it over today with the 'free comrades.'"

I have often wondered what induced B. to take that first step, and could not at once arrive at a conclusion. There was something cunning about him, which prevented me from trusting him entirely, and I imagined that he had in the first place approached us from motives of self-interest. Though we did not put complete trust in him, both my comrades and I tried to convert him to revolutionary ideas. We both took advantage of every opportunity to awaken his better feelings, and to make him an honest and clear-thinking man. Clever and impressionable, like all Little Russians, B. was quickly affected by our propaganda, and it was my lot to witness a curious phenomenon: the regeneration of a man.

I was able to observe him growing every day more serious and thoughtful in his attitude to the cause, and changing from an adroit adventurer into a man of real conviction, ready to face anything to save a comrade. Then my friends outside and I realised that the fitting moment had come for decisive action. I had again to pass my days in the feverish agitation of projects. Increased correspondence took a great deal of energy, as it was greatly complicated by the difficulties of B.'s position.

I have mentioned already that the guard was changed every day.

But there were at the guardhouse, besides the sentinels, porters who performed simply domestic functions. They brought in the dinner and the supper, put out the lamps, and swept the corridors. These porters, six in number, lived permanently at the guard-house, and B. was the chief of them.

But they were forbidden to enter the prisoners' cells except at dinner-time and supper-time, when the sergeant was present. Owing to this circumstance, intercourse with me was extremely difficult, and all B.'s cunning and inventiveness were required to carry on a private correspondence and prolonged conversations with me under such conditions.

The correspondence simply wore me out.

At midnight I would be waked up by a knock, to find the sergeant and B. standing before me with a teapot and boiling water.

"The doctor's assistant ordered you a hot drink at night, didn't he? Here it is for you," he announced to me, and setting the teapot on the table, he deftly slipped a note under it. The door closed, and in spite of my desperate sleepiness I had to begin drinking tea. Then I would wake at dawn for fear of losing a favourable moment for giving B. the reply note. And the whole day was spent in suspense. Not for one minute could one venture on a nap, for fear of missing B. if he came to the door, and at night again I was often expecting a letter from my comrades till two o'clock in the morning.

After a fortnight's correspondence we had several plans of escape sketched out. All might be divided into two classes: those in the execution of which we should have to circumvent all the sentinels, and those in which we should have to depend on the assistance of at least one sentinel.

The former were, of course, attended with considerable risk, and were more complicated; those of the second class were simpler and more certain of success. But the short time the soldiers were on duty made it impossible to win them over to our cause. We therefore made an attempt to carry out one of the first projects.

I have already described how the prisoners were led out to wash in the morning, and how a "good" sergeant would take them out in large batches. The washing basins were in the small corridor (B) adjoining the guards' room. Just opposite the washing place was a small room (A) that served as a storeroom.

Beside the latter was the porters' room.

Owing to the short time they were on duty, the sentinels could not know the porters' faces, and could only tell them by the uniform which they were bound to wear. In that uniform they were free to go in and out of the guard-house. We took advantage of this circumstance to contrive a fairly simple plan of flight.

Taking advantage of his almost unchecked control, B. decided that one morning, when a "good" sergeant would be on duty, he would arrange an airing of the prison beds. For this purpose the prisoners would have to carry their mattresses to the store-room (A), and from there the porters would carry them to the yard of the guard-house, passing on their way through the guards' room, the landing (C) on which a sentinel was always walking to and fro, then a short distance along the street and through the prison gates (D) into the yard. I was to come out with several prisoners to wash, and at the moment when B. would attract the attention of the sentinels by means of some pornographic picture-postcards, I was to go into the store-room (A) and quickly put on the military uniform of a porter, which was to be lying there ready for me, then, putting a mattress on my head, I was to go out into the street, turn the corner, and then run.

We had to wait for the "good" sergeant. But he did not keep us long waiting, and one evening B. told me that the escape was to come off the next morning. Next day the cells of all the prisoners were unlocked at six o'clock, and they went to wash in crowds. My cell, too, was opened. Through the lattice door that separated our corridor (A) from the other corridor (B) I saw the porters carrying out the mattresses, and B. showing the soldiers some picture-postcards. I was ready to go, but B. did not give the signal we had agreed on. I busied myself tidying up my cell, expecting it. B.'s silence surprised me, but it never occurred to me that he could have forgotten the signal. When at last he remembered, it was too late. The sergeant noticed me lingering about, and when at last I went to wash, he sent two sentinels after me.

This failure forced us to try the second plan, which I will now explain. The general idea was the same as before. I was to go out of the guard-house disguised as a porter. But we decided to take advantage of another occasion for attempting this—the moment of extinguishing the street lamps, which was done by the porters between three and four o'clock in the early morning. These lamps stood facing the entrance to the main building and in the yard, where sentinels were always pacing to and fro before the windows of the solitary cells. Disguised as a porter, I could go out into the street on the pretext of extinguishing the lamps in the yard, and, keeping out of the sentinel's

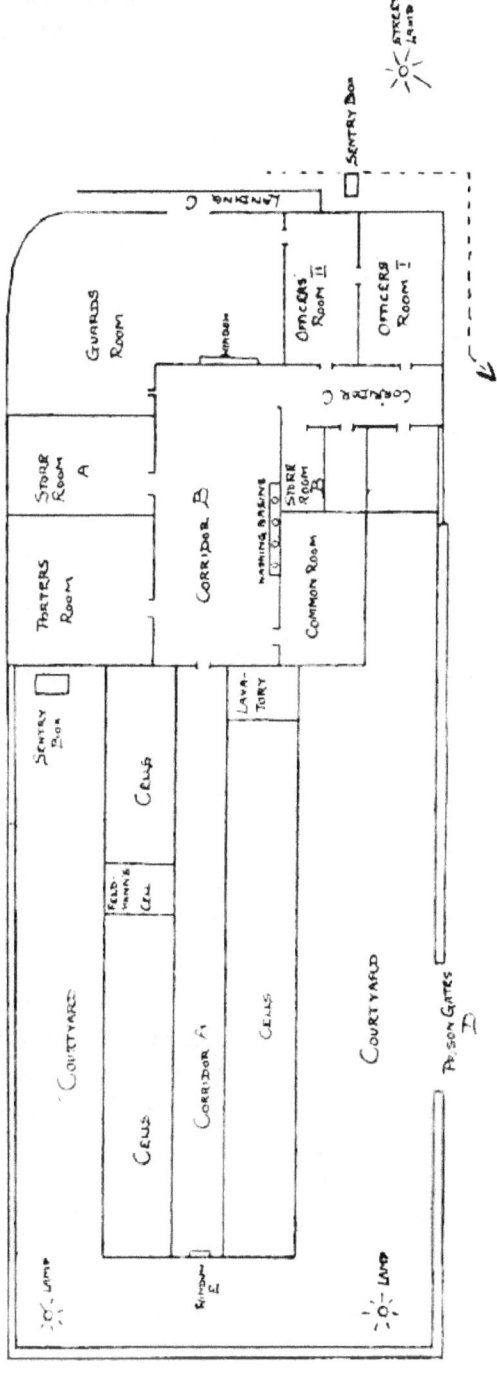

sight, I could walk off to the town in the opposite direction.

At three o'clock in the morning I was to walk out of my cell into corridor A, where my cell was, thence into corridor B, and turning into corridor C, to go into store-room B, and changing my clothes there, to walk to the guards' room, through the officers' room (II), as the door of the latter was close beside the way out of the guard-house, and so I might slip through the guards' room unnoticed.

There were three obstacles in the way of this plan: the sentinel constantly walking up and down corridor A, the lock on the door of my cell, and the officer in the officers' room. But B. very soon got over the two latter difficulties.

One day he plied the sergeant on duty with drink, and while the latter was pouring out the sentiments of his heart, B. took the impression of the key of the solitary cells by means of which my comrades got a new key made. The officers B. circumvented even more simply. Taking advantage of the unbounded confidence put in him, B. declared that for some reason or other the officers' room needed doing up immediately. The staff made arrangements for the room to be done up, and so at night the officers' room was left empty. But though these two difficulties were easily surmounted, the first seemed almost insuperable. To win a sentinel over to our side was impossible, since each man served for one day only, and so it was decided that B. should put the sentinel to sleep by means of specially prepared cigarettes. At first B. took very cordially to the idea, and the comrades prepared the cigarettes, and even made some experiments with them in his presence.

But when it came to action, B. began to draw back, and declared it would be better to wait till we could succeed in getting a sentinel to help us.

B.'s conviction that it was possible to convert a sentinel to our views during his eight hours on duty rested on his faith in the "Hebrews." He imagined that every Jew was in sympathy with the revolution, and that one had but to say one word to get a Jew to act with us.

"There, Kostenka, you wait a bit," he used often to say to me; "as soon as there's a Hebrew on duty at that post! . . . As soon as there is one, you'll get away; don't doubt it. Ah, the Hebrews! they're a golden people!" he would finish, with a gasp of enthusiasm. I doubt whether B. was justified in his faith in the revolutionary character of "Hebrews "in general, but this time his faith was not misplaced. One morning, when, owing to B's having repeatedly put off carrying out his promise to put a sentinel to sleep, we had made up our minds to give up that plan, and were trying to contrive other means of escape, B. came to my cell and said: "Today for the third relief a Hebrew is sentinel; act!"

Having had one experience of treachery with my Pole, and not sharing B.'s belief in the "Hebrews," I took a sceptical view of the position, and resolved inwardly not even to talk to the sentinel. However, when at one o'clock the sentinel of the third relief came on, I went to my door and entered into conversation with him.

"What made you go aboard the *Potemkin*?" he asked me, after I had told him the cause of my arrest.

Then, as far as I could do it, I gave him a strong and succinct picture of the iniquities of contemporary society which had made me a socialist and driven me to take part in the revolution. S. (so I will call the sentinel) listened to me with rapt attention. When I had done, he began—as though unwillingly—telling me of his life as a soldier, and all its dreariness, its humiliation and misery.

"And what they do all this to us for, I don't know. Here my time's up in three months, and they're going, so they say, to pack us off to the war directly. And I'm to go, too. They kill me, and what for? For whose benefit?"

"Why don't you throw up the service?"

"*Ach*, I'd have run away long ago, but I've no money. I don't know a trade either. What am I to do?"

"Well, in that case," I said, feeling that the moment had come for frank and decisive action, "I can help you there, but you must take me with you. Do you agree?"

For the first minute S. was aghast.

"What are you saying! Can you get out from here? Why, this is the tomb! ..."

"Well, that's not the question," I said to him. "The difficulty there is less because we have a trusty friend and assistant here. If you, too, will agree to help me in this business, he will come to you in an hour and tell you the whole plan. And if you think it can be carried out, then help us...."

S. agreed.

Important as S.'s consent was for me, I did not feel that rush of joy I had pictured to myself when imagining this moment beforehand. On the contrary, I felt a great calmness and a sense of the absolute necessity of making an immense effort in those few hours.

"Calm and energy," a voice seemed to be repeating within me, and obeying it, I set to work at once. It was essential to write a note to B.

to explain to him the right tone to take with the soldier. I must think over every detail of the plan and write to my *free* comrades. Among other things I wrote to the latter not to let B. forget to get me shaving materials, boots of the right size, and a belt. The latter article was particularly important, as all prisoners' belts were taken from them, and the lack of one might excite the suspicion of any soldiers I might meet.

I had hardly finished writing these two letters when two soldiers and the sergeant on duty came into my cell.

"Come to exercise," said the sergeant.

But to have to pass unnecessarily through the guards' room, where all the soldiers would see me, did not suit my views, and so, saying that I was unwell, I declined going out at all.

"Only let me have some boiling water," I said to the sergeant, who was delighted at my refusal. A few minutes later B. was in my cell, teapot in hand. At that minute someone gave a shout in the corridor, the sergeant turned, and I seized the moment to give B. the notes. It was four o'clock in the afternoon, and at six B. informed me that S. had finally consented to assist us.

Again, I went over the whole plan; everything had been thought of, and everything was ready. Even a thick coverlet for making a dummy figure of myself had been prepared. There was nothing left for me to do, and there were still nine hours left before the relief in which I was to run away.

"What a long time I have still to sit here," I thought. Thinking it, I remembered that only yesterday I had dreamed with tremor and ecstasy of the chance of long years of penal servitude, only yesterday there had been nothing before me, and today I had a whole lifetime. And to think that I was only separated from life by one door and a grating—a little grating, but life depended on it. Yesterday, today, this moment, it was facing me, torturing me; but tomorrow I should be the other side of it, should think lightly of it, despise it.

Eight o'clock struck.

"Third relief!" I heard shouted.

S. appeared again in the corridor.

"What news?" I asked him.

"Here is a note," S. handed me a note from my friends.

"Everything will be ready," they wrote. "You come out with B.; S. will hand over his duty to another sentinel and come out after you. The comrades will be waiting for you at the bottom of the hill. B. will take you to them. The watchword:—'Be calm and resolute.'"

"Here, see what care our comrades are taking of us," I said to S. "With such friends to help us we cannot doubt of our success."

"I am not afraid," answered S. "Only one thing troubles me: what if your comrades don't wait for me? Where shall I go? I don't know a soul in the town."

"Oh, but that can't happen! The comrades will wait for you," I assured him.

But he was not pacified, and begged me to give him an address he could go to. Yielding to his entreaties, I gave him the address of the lodgings which were the secret meeting-place of our friends. And how thankful I was afterwards that I had done this!

At nine o'clock S.'s shift was over. The sentinel came on duty who would later on follow S. after my escape. He had to be accustomed to the sight of the "dummy," and so I lay down on my bed, and, pulling the coverlet over my head, pretended to go to sleep.

"But I really shall drop asleep." The awful possibility flashed through my mind, but the next minute I laughed at it.

Everything was still, oppressively still, in the guard-house.... Every sound had died down. Only outside the window I could hear the regular tramp of the sentinels, and from time to time the steady sonorous "Listen!" ... the sergeant inspecting the sentinels. The time dragged by, wearisome as the silence itself, and it seemed as though it were standing still, as though the longed-for moment would never come. But at last I heard the tap at the door. I leaped up. S. was standing there.

Again, all weariness had vanished, and the same calm and activity returned to me.

"Get the dummy ready," said S.

With the linen, books, and crockery I had in the cell I made the figure of a man, putting the coverlet over the head. The whole of the previous week I had been practising making this, and so it was so successful that at moments it gave me quite a start of fright when it caught my eye on the bed. It looked so exactly like a man lying there.

"Now I'll open the door and give you the shaving materials," said S., delighted at the lifelike dummy.

But then something awful happened. The key did not fit the lock, and we had only an hour and a half left, and no possibility of making a fresh key.

"Well, how goes it?" I heard the voice of B. from the window (E) leading into the yard.

"The key doesn't fit," said S., going to the window. B. took the key and ran to our comrades, who were keeping watch not far from the guard-house. Happily, there was a working locksmith among them. He promptly filed the key, and when B. brought it back, S. opened the door.

"Now you must come out at once," said S., when I had finished shaving; but at that moment another unexpected obstacle turned up.

That night a "bad" sergeant was on duty, and the soldier prisoners were revenging themselves on him in the one way that was open to them. They prevented him from getting any sleep, by continually asking to leave their cells. And so, at two o'clock at night we heard first one prisoner knocking at the door of his cell, then another, then a third. Now I was again prevented from going out, as the lavatory was in corridor B. and the sergeant was escorting a prisoner there at the moment.

Time was passing, and the prisoners' knocks were unceasing. "Half-past two," S. whispered to me, as he passed my cell. Another half-hour and the game would be lost, and still the knocking kept on.

But in those awful moments my calm did not desert me.

"There are still twenty minutes left. . . . What have I still to do?" I wondered. *Mens sana in corpore sano*; and I had eaten nothing since sunset.

So, I crept to my basket, took out some scraps of provisions, and settled down to supper.

"Fifteen minutes left," I heard S. whisper.

All at once the knocking ceased. For several minutes there was stillness.

"Now go," said S., again opening the door of my cell. I took a step or two towards the door, but all at once I thought of Tchuhnin, through whom I had been transferred there, and was seized with a desire to mock at him. I remembered that my father had left ten *roubles* for me with the staff of the fortress, and of this sum I had spent only sixty *kopecks*. I snatched up a pencil and wrote this note:

"The nine *roubles* forty *kopecks* left with the staff I beg to hand over to Chief Commander Tchuhnin as a tip for kindly transferring me to the military guard-house, and so assisting me to escape."

Laying this note on the table I ran to the storeroom.

I had scarcely reached it when it struck three, and the sentinels were relieved.

I proceeded to put on the soldier's uniform, and at once saw that my reminder about the belt and big boots had not been unnecessary. There was no belt, and the boots would not go on my feet. This broke down my self-possession, and I rushed in a frenzy to B., when he came into the storeroom.

"Oh, don't fret about that; that's a simple matter," he answered, with genuine Little Russian phlegm. "Put on a great coat, as there's no belt, and I'll get the boots in a minute." With that B. walked out. I watched him through the corridor door, wondering where he could possibly get a pair of boots at such an hour. Then I saw my B. walk into the guards' room, and look at the feet of the sleeping soldiers. "That's the thing," I saw on his face, and going up to one of the soldiers, he began pulling off the fellow's boots.

"Wha—at's up?" muttered the man in his heroic sleep; but B. went on undisturbed, and a minute later the boots were on my feet.

"Well, now we'll go," said B. "I've put the sentinel off the scent. Told him I'd a girl coming along to see me from the left side. Gave him a half *rouble* for tea to look out for her. He'll keep his eyes fixed in that direction."

We went into the officers' room. Then I stopped a moment, while B. went ahead. While I went out into the street, he remained standing on the landing.

"Here, take the ladder and go and put them out; first in the yard and then here," B. called aloud to me, pointing to the ladder. I hoisted it at once on to my shoulder, and with a sleepy, deliberate walk I moved towards the corner of the guard-house.

"Look alive, you—" here followed some round Russian oaths. "What's awry with your stumps?"

I quickened my pace a little . . . and in a moment I had passed out of sight of the sentinel.

Only then I felt that I was in freedom. . . . The breath of freedom and of life seemed to embrace me, and everything in me responded to that caress.

Then I heard steps behind me. It was B. running. Till that moment he had acted with amazing coolness; now he had suddenly lost all self-control.

"We must run, Kostenka," he cried, and seizing me by the arm, began racing downhill with me. In vain I tried to calm him, and to persuade him to walk quietly, pointing out the danger of being noticed. Chased by demons, B. dragged me on and on. He only stopped when we had run far beyond the place where our comrades were to wait for us, and when we went back, they were not there.

"Well, now what are we to do?" cried B., clutching his head.

"Don't you know some address?" I asked him.

"No."

"Where's the lodging where you used to meet the comrades?"

"You can't go there in a soldier's uniform; there are policemen standing there."

And indeed, I had no belt on, and any constable might arrest me for my uniform not being in order.

"Do you know anyone at whose rooms I could change my clothes?"

But B. had quite lost his head, and for a whole hour he dragged me on through dark and dirty streets. At last he bethought himself of something.

"To be sure, I know of some good people," he said; "let's go to them." And he began taking me to his "good people."

First, he conducted me to a crony of his, a *dvornik*. The man at once saw something was amiss and wanted to arrest us. Action was necessary. I gave him a box on one ear with all my force, B. gave him one on the other, and the crony fell unconscious on the ground.

Then we fastened the door of his room on the outside and decamped.

The second "good man" to whom B. took me turned out to be a soldier of the watch. He simply turned us away; but I did get a belt from him. Meanwhile it was daylight and the moment was approaching when my disappearance must be discovered at the guard-house.

"Well, now we'll go to the comrades," I said resolutely, hailing a cabman. Even then B. was obstinate, and kept urging that we should go to a cookshop to think over our position.

My firmness prevailed, and we took a cab. A few turnings before reaching the lodging we stopped the driver.

"Pay him," I said.

As ill-luck would have it, B. only had two five *rouble* pieces, and one of these he gave the man.

"I've no change!"

"And I have nothing else. . . ."

"Well, get change then—"

But all the shops were still shut. We tried to get change from passers-by, but in vain. Meanwhile, we were beginning to attract the attention of the street; every moment we lingered was dangerous. What were we to do? To give the man the five *roubles* would be to excite his suspicions at once. I tried guile. With the time-honoured stage gesture, I scratched my head, and addressing the driver, said:

"Come, mate, give us the change. We've been out on the spree, as you see, and by now the officer'll be up. You see, we poor soldier chaps—"

"But I haven't got it, I tell you straight," the man interrupted.

"Well, what's one to do, then? We can't stay. You take the five *roubles* and tell us where your stand is. I'll come to you for the change. You'll give it us all right?"

Even then the cabman protested.

"I don't want your money. Maybe you'll be saying after that it was ten or twenty you gave me. Give me my sixty *kopecks* and be off!"

I had much ado to persuade him to let us go.

The gates of the house where the comrades lived were already open, and the *dvornik* was sweeping the street. Watching our moment when he had turned away, we whisked into the yard unseen by him. The door to the staircase on which were the comrades' rooms was locked. Then we lost patience, and shoved at the door with such force that it gave way, and in a moment, we had our comrades all round us. Then we began undressing and dressing up. All at once they caught a glimpse of a soldier's coat on the stairs, and there was a ring at the bell.

"A police raid!" cried the comrades, and they hid us. But a timid, almost supplicating voice in the entry made me come out of hiding, and the Jewish soldier S. rushed sobbing to me.

At three o'clock in the night he had brought the soldier who relieved him to the door of my cell, and, pointing out the dummy figure, had handed him over his post. He had remained at the guard-house till dawn, and then slipped away and set off into the town.

Meanwhile the comrades, after waiting an extra hour for me in vain, had concluded that the plan had not come off, and so had gone home. Not finding them at the appointed place, S. was terrified. He thought he was the victim of a deception. Filled with the most dreadful doubts, he made for the address I had given him . . . and his face and his voice were full of horror, as he described what he felt before getting there.

We spent several days in Sevastopol. The search took place before my very eyes. The comrades told me that the whole port and the railway-station were surrounded by a cordon of troops, and the strictest watch was kept on all travellers. The whole town was in a turmoil over the escape, and Tchuhnin was in a fury. I happened to overhear a Sevastopol police-inspector describing how Tchuhnin had sent for him, had stamped with rage, and ordered him to find all the fugitives that very day.

"If you don't find them, I'll put you all under arrest!" the admiral had shouted in his wrath.

"And how's one to find them? They've got to Roumania long ago, you may be sure," the police inspector added dolefully, not suspecting that I was so close to him.

It happened to me, indeed, several times to have "Feldmann's clever escape" described to me. I remember one scene in particular in a Russian town three weeks after my escape.

I was staying in the house of a Liberal government official, but neither he nor the other members of his household knew my real name. One morning a young lady of their acquaintance ran into the room where I was, and almost screamed: "Have you heard? . . . They have caught Feldmann!"

"What are you telling us?" I cried, with pretended horror and incredulity. "Surely that can't be true!"

"But here's the telegram in the paper!" said the girl; and, her hands trembling with excitement, she showed me in the newspaper the telegram about the capture of Feldmann at one of the frontier stations. I was going to say how sorry I was for Feldmann, but the young girl was so distressed that I hastened to soothe her. "The telegram might be wrong; newspapers often make such things up," I assured her.

My exit from Sevastopol took place in luxurious style. In a handsome landau drawn by four fine horses, a festive party, consisting of a fashionably-dressed young lady, a personage of very high position in Sevastopol, B., and me, drove out of the town. We were singing, making jokes, and laughing. Nobody could have guessed that in such a party there were men threatened with the death penalty. , . .

We had scarcely driven out of the town, when all at once I cried out involuntarily: "The captain of the watch! . . ."

There came riding on horseback straight towards us an officer, who had been on duty at the guardhouse the week before my escape.

But an outburst of laughter from my companions covered my exclamation, and the officer, noticing no embarrassment, and not recognising me, rode calmly by, positively smiling at our hilarity.

This incident made us change places. I sat with my back to the horses, and H. (so I will call the person of high position) sat in my place.

"It's better so," said H. "As soon as those scoundrels see me, they'll turn away."

This precaution was not thrown away, as within a few minutes we met a sergeant, and an hour later B. recognised the horse of a captain. All these worthy gentlemen, though they were undoubtedly looking for us, could not imagine we should be driving in an open landau in broad daylight. It was a great help, too, having H. with us. At the sight of him, all the very men we had to fear stood at attention, and flew with bewildering swiftness to carry out his orders. I remember that at one halting-place a police officer tried to peer into our carriage.

It was clear from his air that he had some suspicion, and had determined to get a good look at us. I whispered to H., and he promptly got out of the carriage and confronted the police officer. Seeing him, the latter drew himself up, saluted, and, as though afraid H. guessed his evil intent—of peeping into the carriage—he retired with rapid steps.

So, we drove to Simferopol. Here I parted from B., and he travelled by another road. He joined S. at a certain town, and they both crossed the frontier successfully.

I moved about Russia for another month. Several amusing incidents occurred to me in the course of this perilous wandering, as I very often had to come into contact with the authorities, but I hoodwinked them successfully.

I reached the frontier accompanied by a comrade of much experience in smuggling matters. We were met at a little frontier town by a smuggler to whom we had telegraphed beforehand. In his company we got into a conveyance that stood ready for us, and set off to a little place situated about thirty *versts* from the frontier. Here, in a dirty little house, we had to wait till evening. It was a typical smuggler's nest. We had hardly entered the best room, which rather suggested the den of some wild beast, when a perfect crowd of healthy young lads—the smuggler's children—came trooping in. They had grown up in an atmosphere of danger and secrecy, and were as crafty and tricky as their calling itself.

"What news? How's business?" they fell upon my companion, who was evidently an old friend. While they were talking to him, their father, the old smuggler came in. His large nose, piercing gaze, and light catlike movements made him like some beast of prey. Forty years of dangerous enterprises had left a distinct mark upon the man.

"When are we setting off?" my companion asked him.

"At nine o'clock. . . . A political?" the old man queried in his turn, scanning me with his searching eyes.

My comrade, being anxious not to excite the smuggler's suspicions, and to manage this crossing even more secretly than usual, gave out that I was his partner travelling with a large consignment of goods.

"We are getting several dozen *poods* of goods across through you," he said; "but it must be done without delay; the whole business must be finished within the week. And so please manage today's crossing so that there may be no stoppages."

"In that case I'll go with you myself," said the old man.

At nine o'clock we were led through a door into a dark stable. The horses stood ready in the cart.

"Ready?" asked the driver, when we had clambered in.

"With God's blessing," said the old man. "Drive on, and I'll overtake you at the pond."

"Why do they take such precautions even here?" I asked my companion.

He explained that crossing the actual frontier presented no difficulty or danger for these smugglers, as the very soldiers and *gendarmes* who are put there to guard the frontier, carry the contraband goods across. But the road to the frontier was full of danger, as there were frequent patrols for twenty *versts* from the frontier. These patrol-men had not been bought off, and arrested people on the slightest suspicion.

At the appointed spot we found the old man waiting for us in a little one-horse cart with one of his sons. We drove in a peculiar, silent way to the frontier, a little village.

"Wait here," said the old man, and he drove on ahead of us.

We could see him stop, get out of his cart, and walk on. Ten minutes later he came back and said that the *gendarme* was not at the place agreed on. "Wait here a little, I'll look again," he said, and like a cat he vanished into the darkness.

Half an hour passed. . . . We were standing in the most dangerous place. Any minute a patrol might pass. It was natural that phantoms should begin to hover round us, and all at once my comrade said to me:

"Let us hide in the hollow."

We climbed warily out of the cart and crept down into some sort of a hole. There we lay for a full hour. At last the old man reappeared.

"We must go back; the *gendarme's* played us false and not turned up," he said.

We had to drive through all the dangerous parts again. At three o'clock in the morning we got back to the same little house.

Thoroughly exhausted we fell into a sound sleep as soon as we lay down on our beds. Next morning the old man sent his son to warn another *gendarme* of our passing that night.

That very day all the police of the little place were on the alert. Six men crossing from Austria had been caught the previous evening, but four of them had run away. There were police posted on all the roads, and it was only through the experience and cunning of the old man that we succeeded in passing them.

At midnight we reached the frontier.

The *gendarme* was already waiting for us, but he told us we could only cross the frontier at three o'clock. A tarpaulin was spread on the ground for us, and lying down on it we had to wait for the time when we could cross. It was pouring with rain, and desperately cold and damp. . . . Huddling together, we tried to keep warm. . . .

Precisely at three o'clock in the morning a frontier soldier and the *gendarme* came up to us. The latter shouldered our trunks, and we started. Soon we saw the road shining white before us. The soldier halted, handed the *gendarme* his gun, took our things from him, and saying, "This is the frontier, try not to leave traces," moved on ahead...

In a moment we were over the frontier of the Austrian Empire.

Appendix

The Story of the Rescue Told by One of the Author's Comrades

We, the comrades of the Social Democrat organisation, were in Odessa, when we heard from Kirill of Feldmann's arrest at Theodosia. Although everyone was in terror after the days of massacre in Odessa, and people shrank away in horror at the very word "revolution," we succeeded in two days in collecting the funds necessary for attempting to save him from the gallows. At the same time a comrade of the Rostov Committee of the Social Democrats went to Theodosia to investigate the position. Besides the Odessa Committee, members of the Bund, and of the Kiev Committee, and I need hardly say also, of the Crimea Committee, which, being on the spot, took a leading part, were associated in our enterprise. From Theodosia we heard immediately that Feldmann had been moved to Sevastopol, and two comrades set off there at once.

Another comrade, a woman, devoted herself entirely to the attempt, and though she remained in Odessa, she took the most active part in working out the details of the plan, and sending what persons or things were needed to Sevastopol. She was the moving spirit who urged us on and kept us all at work. I myself went to Sevastopol; another of us was sent to Berlin, where he obtained a thousand marks from a sympathetic German Liberal. In Sevastopol we found an old comrade, a workman who showed great knowledge of human nature, experience, and courage in helping us.

The comrade from Rostov, whom we will call X., was a very vigorous and cool-headed person. Before I arrived, he had managed in an incredibly short time to get into communication with the prison, and we entered upon a lively correspondence with Feldmann. Not a day passed without our exchanging letter by the so-called "pigeon-post." Everything went smoothly. We concocted an excellent plan, which must have succeeded if Admiral Tchuhnin had not unluckily transferred Feldmann to the guard-house.

What made it so horrible was that it was only two days before our plan was to be carried out that this transfer took place. It was a knockdown blow for us. All our efforts, all our schemes were destroyed at one stroke. We had to begin all over again from the beginning.

To get into relation with the soldiers of the guardhouse was our problem now. Was it possible? Were there any means by which we could do this? We rushed to the Sevastopol Committee of our organisation.

"Have you any connections of any sort with the guard-house?"

"No."

"Not the slightest acquaintance with one wretched soldier?"

"No, none. The soldiers at the guard-house are not always the same; they are changed every day, and are taken from different regiments."

It was awful. Already several days of July had passed, and we learned that the investigation was going on at a great pace, and would shortly be over.

Death was close upon us. It was already hanging over our comrade. What could we do?

We made plans, each one more fantastic, more reckless than the other, and in this very recklessness we saw our own impotence.

From this helpless position we were rescued by comrade Feldmann himself. He somehow succeeded in securing the services of the senior porter, B.

On one of our gloomiest days a girl, one of our comrades, whose address had been given to Feldmann before he was transferred, ran in, crying:

"Come, come, quick! A soldier from the guardhouse is at my rooms!"

"A soldier! From the guard-house! You don't mean it!"

"Yes, come, come! He can't wait!"

We rushed at lightning speed.

We arranged beforehand that only one of us should see the soldier; the other one was to stay in the next room, to be ready to advise at any moment.

Comrade T. saw a puny little man, evidently a Little Russian from his appearance, who handed him a note consisting of the following two words:

"Send greetings."

Evidently this was by way of a first trial of our communications.

"Who are you?" asked T.

"I am a soldier."

"Are you from the guard-house? Are you permanently there?"

"Yes, I am the senior porter."

"That's first-rate. Can you take a note to Feldmann? You shall be well rewarded."

"Why not? Write it."

We felt we were clutching at a straw. Still, we had to put him to the test, to see what manner of man he was. How could we tell he would not betray us?

We sent a note of the same content—"Our greetings"—and gave a *rouble* to B., asking him to bring us another note, if possible.

And so, the correspondence continued.

Next day B. received a second *rouble*, and, though he declared he was not acting for the sake of money, he was naturally pleased, and suggested that he could bring us notes two or three times a day. We accepted his offer, of course.

It is an interesting question, What induced B. to come to our help? It is difficult to say. He was certainly not a convinced revolutionist, but the universal atmosphere of sympathy with the revolutionary movement affected him. He had begun to realise that everything was not quite as it should be in the old *régime*. Then he was interested in Feldmann, as one of the heroes of the *Potemkin*,

Mercenary considerations no doubt entered partly into his reckoning—partly, I say, for he would never have done what he did for his personal interest only.

With his help we exchanged notes two or three times a day with Feldmann.

The Sevastopol police is a somewhat primitive organisation. They have no spies, and, being aware of this, we were not afraid to meet B. always at the same lodging. But as a precaution we kept one of our comrades on the look-out in the street, and this gave rise to an amusing misunderstanding. Of the Sevastopol group of Social Democrats, only a few, of course, were aware of the attempt we were making. It happened that the group arranged a meeting in the very same house in which we were in the habit of meeting B. During an interview with B., a girl comrade, was on sentinel duty for us in the street. The Social Democrats, who were on their way to the meeting, observed this girl watching the house, and, taking her for a spy, put off the meeting. Next day all the members of the party could talk of nothing else, and were full of the news that the police had taken to employing female spies.

Later on we gave up meeting always at the same spot, and met in all sorts of unlikely places—while bathing in the sea, for instance.

To give a clear picture of the conditions under which we lived, I must describe another episode. We were, of course, all living under false names, and with false passports. Comrade T. alone had a good real passport, belonging to a University graduate. In order to avoid showing it to the police, however, T. stayed at an hotel, whose proprietor had all the police in his pay. Many Jews, visiting the town for a few days, stayed at his hotel, to avoid the persecution of the police, arising from the restrictions under which they are placed.

The owner of the hotel was rather puzzled that T., having such an excellent passport, should have come to his hotel, and he asked him what had induced him to stay there. He answered that, being a Jew himself, he preferred to patronise a compatriot, knowing what expense he was put to with the police. This answer quite satisfied the hotel-keeper.

For a time, I lived in the house of a schoolmistress; but I did not like exposing her to danger, and besides, I knew from experience that it was wise to change our lodging pretty frequently. The keeper of the hotel where T. lodged used to bolt the outer door every night, and a quarter of an hour later he would be fast asleep. Then I used to approach T.'s window and give a cautious whistle, and he would come down very quietly with bare feet, and would let me in. Both of us would creep up like thieves to his room.

The hotel was a wretched place at the best. One of us had to sleep on three chairs without a pillow, as there was only one bed, and that a very narrow one. In the morning we went through a regular comedy. At six I was let out, the landlord being still asleep, and at seven o'clock I knocked at the door and asked to see my friend again. So, it went on, day after day. The end of July was near. We were terribly exhausted by the nervous strain of our existence. The nights were awful, and during the day we had nothing to do except to interview B., and to discuss our plans. We did not dare to visit friends for fear of compromising them. To walk up and down the streets was a source of danger. We were on a continual strain, and yet we had to keep cool and think of every detail. The sea was what saved us.

We studied the plan of the guard-house, and knew every detail of the building, but we had little hope of success. B. concocted a number of schemes, but they were all quite fantastic, and would not stand a moment's serious criticism.

But when B. decided to escape himself with the prisoner, our hopes rose higher. The following plan was made: a skeleton key was to be obtained, and the help of a sentinel to be secured, or, failing this, a sleeping-draught was to be administered to one of the sentinels. The door was to be opened; a dummy figure was to be made of the blankets; Feldmann was to sleep with the blanket over his head for several nights, to familiarise the gaolers with the appearance of the dummy; then Feldmann, dressed as a soldier, was to leave the cell with B., and they were to go out together into the yard to turn out the lamps, and then into the street, where we were to be waiting for them.

This plan was carried out most perfectly, but its accomplishment cost us a terrible expenditure of nerves and energy.

At the critical moment B. would put off carrying out the plan. One day he would fancy there were suspicious people about; another day he would be unable to provide some article of the soldier's uniform required. All this was terribly wearing for us. Every night we had to be on the watch near the guard-house, and all the while in expectation and suspense.

A rustle.... They are coming! ... One's heart is in one's mouth. ..., A soldier passes....

Again, a rustle ... again footsteps ... two men are seen.... It is they! ... No, it is not they!

And so, night after night.

And all the while we had to be on our guard that passers-by should not notice us.

Sometimes we had to lie flat on the ground, or to hide under a fence to escape observation.

A serious difficulty was to secure a lodging for Feldmann and B., in which they could lie hidden after their escape.

We were afraid to speak, even to sympathisers, of the proposed escape before it had taken place, for fear of its being talked about. And so, on the eve of one of the nights fixed for the escape, I went to a householder, of whom I was told that he would not refuse us a shelter if we told him the truth.

I arrived, and was received very politely by the gentleman in question.

I presented my introduction and explained the position: "Give us a hiding-place for Feldmann, whose escape we have arranged."

"But it's impossible! How can you rescue him from a military prison?"

I convinced him of the facts.

"When will it be?" he asked.

"Tonight."

The gentleman gazed at me with wide-open eyes; then he stammered out:

"I m af—f—fraid!"

That settled it!

Then he began excusing himself, talking of a police-search that had taken place ten years before, and so on.

I exacted secrecy on his word of honour, and, having received bushels of good advice, I left him, no better off than when I came.

The situation was tragic.

The local comrades explained that it was impossible to get rooms. Everyone was in terror, and the only chance, they said, was for the fugitives to leave the town at once.

Then a bright idea occurred to me.

I am sorry to say I had to tell a lie to carry it out.

Feldmann, as he wrote to us, had grown a tremendous beard in prison, and he wanted to shave, which would alter his appearance and make him look much younger. So, suppose we were to dress him for the first few days as a sixth-form high-school boy? A boy of that age would have a better chance of finding a refuge. People would not believe that a schoolboy could be very seriously compromised.

The following conversation took place with a doctor to whom we appealed:

"Doctor, couldn't you put up a sixth-form boy, who's coming with the message from the Odessa organisation, for a couple of nights?"

"A high-school boy?"

"Yes."

"Why doesn't he go to an hotel?"

"Ah, you see an hotel's not quite convenient for a schoolboy. First, it might attract the notice of the police; secondly, he is away without leave; and then he's a Jew besides, and has no right of residence in Sevastopol."

"Oh, very well. He may spend a couple of nights here; but let me tell you, this is just why people are not more ready to give you Social Democrats their support and subscriptions, because you include so many little boys and girls in your party. What confidence can we put in a party that sends schoolboys with revolutionary messages!"

His Social Democrat listener had to swallow this with a contrite smile.

The second day that the schoolboy stayed with the doctor the latter began to have an inkling of the truth. The whole town, of course, was talking of nothing but Feldmann's escape; and he simply asked the "schoolboy" to move on as soon as possible.

A few months later our doctor, meeting in Moscow an old acquaintance, a member of our party, boasted of the great service he had done the revolutionary cause, and related how gladly he had hidden Feldmann after his escape.

So is history written.

B. had managed to make a model of the key, which was kept by the senior sergeant on duty. And we had a key made from the model. All this was done in one day. The shaving-materials were sent to Feldmann, and the schoolboy's uniform was ready.

Now we had to make experiments with the sleeping-draught.

One of our comrades, a broad-shouldered, sturdy fellow, a chemist, who had been specially summoned from the Volga and took a leading part in arranging the rescue, tried the drug on himself. Two of us were present, and a terrible experience we had. The sleeping-draught turned out to be too efficacious, and the comrade fell into a swoon from which we only succeeded with difficulty in restoring him at last, by means of cold water, coffee, and compresses.

After this experiment B. showed an insurmountable reluctance to use the sleeping-draught, and it was fortunately not needed.

At last everything was ready.

On the night fixed two of the comrades were again on the watch in the street, while I had to be at the doctor's to receive the "schoolboy." The hour fixed was between half-past one and three. This hour and a half seemed endless. The excitement was intense. The watchers' nerves were strained to the utmost limit.

"They are running!"

Two men ran by very quickly. They flew after them, but could not overtake them.

"Then it could not have been they! They would not have run by the appointed place! They wouldn't pass their own friends!"

There stood the watchers still, waiting! Three o'clock passed . . . half-past three.

The comrades came back exhausted and despondent.

Once more . . . nothing! It was awful!

At seven o'clock in the morning I went to an appointment by the sea. There friends were waiting to see me.

"Again, a failure—damn it!" I said.

"Sh! . . . they are safe!"

"What! Was it they, then, who ran by the comrades so quickly?"

"Yes! Tell us what to do! Quickly!"

At last all three, then, were free.

What we still had to do seemed very easy, and yet it was the most difficult part of the whole business! To get them out of the town!

The Sevastopol railway runs in a single line for about twelve hours' journey.

We wanted to separate them, but, after all, B. had to travel with Feldmann as far as Simferopol.

The first to get away was the Jewish sentinel. We provided a wife and baby for him, and carrying the latter in his arms he did not excite suspicion. Feldmann and B. remained some time longer. They had to be sent away on a different plan. B. dyed his hair and beard, so that his own friends could not recognise him. Feldmann also disguised himself, and they set off together, driving in a private carriage with two other persons.

At last they reached Simferopol.

Here we found true citizens, who were not afraid to shelter the fugitives. In the latter part of his journey Feldmann travelled as the son of a rich lady. I cannot refrain from expressing my admiration of the pluck of this lady. She undertook the journey simply because she knew whom she was helping, and she showed the greatest public spirit and courage. I have no more to add, except that we deeply regretted that our attempts to rescue other comrades of the *Potemkin* were unsuccessful. To the best of my belief, as much energy and more money was spent on these attempts, but all were in vain.

The Russian revolution has furnished a whole series of instances of escapes, sometimes of single individuals, sometimes of a number at once, from remote Siberia, from prisons, and from penal settlements. The future historians of the revolution cannot pass by these rescues, which constitute a chapter of the history of the Great Russian Revolution.

ALSO FROM LEONAUR
AVAILABLE IN SOFTCOVER OR HARDCOVER WITH DUST JACKET

THE FALL OF THE MOGHUL EMPIRE OF HINDUSTAN by H. G. Keene—By the beginning of the nineteenth century, as British and Indian armies under Lake and Wellesley dominated the scene, a little over half a century of conflict brought the Moghul Empire to its knees.

LADY SALE'S AFGHANISTAN by Florentia Sale—An Indomitable Victorian Lady's Account of the Retreat from Kabul During the First Afghan War.

THE CAMPAIGN OF MAGENTA AND SOLFERINO 1859 by Harold Carmichael Wylly—The Decisive Conflict for the Unification of Italy.

FRENCH'S CAVALRY CAMPAIGN by J. G. Maydon—A Special Correspondent's View of British Army Mounted Troops During the Boer War.

CAVALRY AT WATERLOO by Sir Evelyn Wood—British Mounted Troops During the Campaign of 1815.

THE SUBALTERN by George Robert Gleig—The Experiences of an Officer of the 85th Light Infantry During the Peninsular War.

NAPOLEON AT BAY, 1814 by F. Loraine Petre—The Campaigns to the Fall of the First Empire.

NAPOLEON AND THE CAMPAIGN OF 1806 by Colonel Vachée—The Napoleonic Method of Organisation and Command to the Battles of Jena & Auerstädt.

THE COMPLETE ADVENTURES IN THE CONNAUGHT RANGERS by William Grattan—The 88th Regiment during the Napoleonic Wars by a Serving Officer.

BUGLER AND OFFICER OF THE RIFLES by William Green & Harry Smith—With the 95th (Rifles) during the Peninsular & Waterloo Campaigns of the Napoleonic Wars.

NAPOLEONIC WAR STORIES by Sir Arthur Quiller-Couch—Tales of soldiers, spies, battles & sieges from the Peninsular & Waterloo campaingns.

CAPTAIN OF THE 95TH (RIFLES) by Jonathan Leach—An officer of Wellington's sharpshooters during the Peninsular, South of France and Waterloo campaigns of the Napoleonic wars.

RIFLEMAN COSTELLO by Edward Costello—The adventures of a soldier of the 95th (Rifles) in the Peninsular & Waterloo Campaigns of the Napoleonic wars.

AVAILABLE ONLINE AT www.leonaur.com
AND FROM ALL GOOD BOOK STORES

ALSO FROM LEONAUR
AVAILABLE IN SOFTCOVER OR HARDCOVER WITH DUST JACKET

A DIARY FROM DIXIE *by Mary Boykin Chesnut*—A Lady's Account of the Confederacy During the American Civil War

FOLLOWING THE DRUM *by Teresa Griffin Vielé*—A U. S. Infantry Officer's Wife on the Texas frontier in the Early 1850's

FOLLOWING THE GUIDON *by Elizabeth B. Custer*—The Experiences of General Custer's Wife with the U. S. 7th Cavalry.

LADIES OF LUCKNOW *by G. Harris & Adelaide Case*—The Experiences of Two British Women During the Indian Mutiny 1857. A Lady's Diary of the Siege of Lucknow by G. Harris, Day by Day at Lucknow by Adelaide Case

MARIE-LOUISE AND THE INVASION OF 1814 *by Imbert de Saint-Amand*—The Empress and the Fall of the First Empire

SAPPER DOROTHY *by Dorothy Lawrence*—The only English Woman Soldier in the Royal Engineers 51st Division, 79th Tunnelling Co. during the First World War

ARMY LETTERS FROM AN OFFICER'S WIFE 1871-1888 *by Frances M. A. Roe*—Experiences On the Western Frontier With the United States Army

NAPOLEON'S LETTERS TO JOSEPHINE *by Henry Foljambe Hall*—Correspondence of War, Politics, Family and Love 1796-1814

MEMOIRS OF SARAH DUCHESS OF MARLBOROUGH, AND OF THE COURT OF QUEEN ANNE VOLUME 1 by A. T. Thomson

MEMOIRS OF SARAH DUCHESS OF MARLBOROUGH, AND OF THE COURT OF QUEEN ANNE VOLUME 2 by A. T. Thomson

MARY PORTER GAMEWELL AND THE SIEGE OF PEKING *by A. H. Tuttle*—An American Lady's Experiences of the Boxer Uprising, China 1900

VANISHING ARIZONA *by Martha Summerhayes*—A young wife of an officer of the U.S. 8th Infantry in Apacheria during the 1870's

THE RIFLEMAN'S WIFE *by Mrs. Fitz Maurice*—*The Experiences of an Officer's Wife and Chronicles of the Old 95th During the Napoleonic Wars*

THE OATMAN GIRLS *by Royal B. Stratton*—The Capture & Captivity of Two Young American Women in the 1850's by the Apache Indians

---

AVAILABLE ONLINE AT **www.leonaur.com**
AND FROM ALL GOOD BOOK STORES

ALSO FROM LEONAUR
AVAILABLE IN SOFTCOVER OR HARDCOVER WITH DUST JACKET

ESCAPE FROM THE FRENCH *by Edward Boys*—A Young Royal Navy Midshipman's Adventures During the Napoleonic War.

THE VOYAGE OF H.M.S. PANDORA *by Edward Edwards R. N. & George Hamilton, edited by Basil Thomson*—In Pursuit of the Mutineers of the Bounty in the South Seas—1790-1791.

MEDUSA *by J. B. Henry Savigny and Alexander Correard and Charlotte-Adélaïde Dard*—Narrative of a Voyage to Senegal in 1816 & The Sufferings of the Picard Family After the Shipwreck of the Medusa.

THE SEA WAR OF 1812 VOLUME 1 *by A. T. Mahan*—A History of the Maritime Conflict.

THE SEA WAR OF 1812 VOLUME 2 *by A. T. Mahan*—A History of the Maritime Conflict.

WETHERELL OF H. M. S. HUSSAR *by John Wetherell*—The Recollections of an Ordinary Seaman of the Royal Navy During the Napoleonic Wars.

THE NAVAL BRIGADE IN NATAL *by C. R. N. Burne*—With the Guns of H. M. S. Terrible & H. M. S. Tartar during the Boer War 1899-1900.

THE VOYAGE OF H. M. S. BOUNTY *by William Bligh*—The True Story of an 18th Century Voyage of Exploration and Mutiny.

SHIPWRECK! *by William Gilly*—The Royal Navy's Disasters at Sea 1793-1849.

KING'S CUTTERS AND SMUGGLERS: 1700-1855 *by E. Keble Chatterton*—A unique period of maritime history-from the beginning of the eighteenth to the middle of the nineteenth century when British seamen risked all to smuggle valuable goods from wool to tea and spirits from and to the Continent.

CONFEDERATE BLOCKADE RUNNER *by John Wilkinson*—The Personal Recollections of an Officer of the Confederate Navy.

NAVAL BATTLES OF THE NAPOLEONIC WARS *by W. H. Fitchett*—Cape St. Vincent, the Nile, Cadiz, Copenhagen, Trafalgar & Others.

PRISONERS OF THE RED DESERT *by R. S. Gwatkin-Williams*—The Adventures of the Crew of the Tara During the First World War.

U-BOAT WAR 1914-1918 *by James B. Connolly/Karl von Schenk*—Two Contrasting Accounts from Both Sides of the Conflict at Sea D uring the Great War.

AVAILABLE ONLINE AT **www.leonaur.com**
AND FROM ALL GOOD BOOK STORES

www.ingramcontent.com/pod-product-compliance
Lightning Source LLC
Chambersburg PA
CBHW022006100426
42738CB00041B/492